ANNA DEL CONTE'S
ITALIAN KITCHEN
ILLUSTRATED BY FLO BAYLEY

ANNA DEL CONTE'S
ITALIAN KITCHEN

ILLUSTRATED BY FLO BAYLEY

PAVILION

This edition published in Great Britain in 1995 by
PAVILION BOOKS LIMITED
26 Upper Ground, London SE1 9PD

Originally published as four separate volumes in 1993

Designed by Andrew Barron & Collis Clements Associates
Gli Antipasti
La Pasta
I Risotti
I Dolce

Jacket designed by Bernard Higton

A CIP catalogue record for this book is available from the
British Library

ISBN 1 85793 614 0

Printed and bound in Italy by New Interlitho, Milan

2 4 6 8 10 9 7 5 3 1

This book may be ordered by post direct from the publisher.
Please contact the Marketing Department.
But try your bookshop first.

CONTENTS

GLI ANTIPASTI

When I was taken out to dinner as a child I only ate *l'antipasto*. The trolley would be wheeled next to me and I would be transfixed by the beauty of the food and bewildered by the choice. After a few decades I still feel like that. I want to take all the dishes home, admire them, and eat them slowly and thoughtfully over the next few days. First a taste of prosciutto, as well as culatello and felino, my favourite salami, which I would eat with bread and nothing else. Next would come a few floppy slices of grilled peppers, a curly tentacle of *calameretti*, and a morsel of each stuffed vegetable. Finally, a spoonful of *nervetti in insalata* – Milanese brawn – gleaming with olive oil and crowned with colourful *sottaceti* – vegetables preserved in vinegar – and speckled with purple olives and miniscule green capers.

Such are the delights of an antipasto offered in a restaurant. When you serve antipasti at home, however, you must be more selective and decide on two or three dishes at most. Otherwise you will be in the kitchen for far too long and begin to hate the idea of an antipasto for ever.

An antipasto can provide a good beginning to a meal, and it can even set the style for the meal itself. It is very important that, as an opening to the meal, it should be well presented and pretty to look at. It should also be light and fresh, so as to develop the taste buds for the courses to follow, rather than fill the stomach, and it should harmonise with the rest of the meal.

Nowadays an antipasto is usually a starter, no longer followed by a *primo* – first course – except on special occasions. For instance, if you have decided on a platter of *affettato misto* – mixed cured meats – a generous bowl of tagliatelle dressed with a vigorous sauce would make an ideal follow-on. So also would an earthy risotto or a gutsy spaghetti *alla puttanesca* – with tomatoes, anchovies and chilli. This is not the traditional Italian way, but it is what suits our smaller stomachs and the preachings of the health gurus.

If, however, you are serving a joint of meat, start with a vegetable-based antipasto or a fish one. A fish antipasto, indeed, is the ideal precursor to a fish main course.

The recipes collected here are divided into six sections: Salumi, Various Salads, Fish and Meat Antipasti, Stuffed Vegetables, Crostini and Bruschetta, and Other Favourites. Some of the recipes are for classic antipasto dishes, others are my own or those of my family and friends. All are typically Italian yet very varied. As varied, indeed, as most Italian cooking, because of the great differences between its many regions.

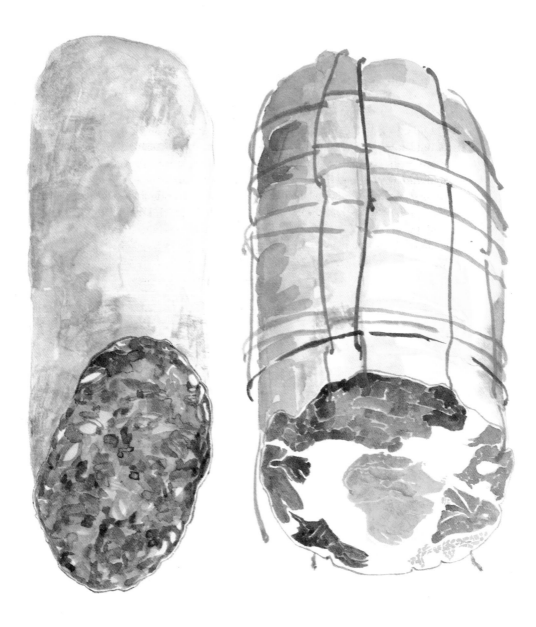

SALUMI

CURED MEAT PRODUCTS

Iknow I am an unashamed chauvinist where food is concerned, but I am sure no other country offers such an array of delectable cured meats as Italy does. Salumi are usually made with pork or a mixture of pork and beef. There are also good salumi made with venison and various other meats. The mocetta from Valle d'Aosta is made with wild goat, the bresaola from Valtellina with fillet of beef, the salame d'oca from Friuli and Veneto with goose, and the salami and prosciutti di cinghiale are made with wild boar. This latter is one of the many glories of Tuscany.

The characteristics of the many types of salumi are determined firstly by factors affecting the pig, or other animal, itself. These include its breed, its habitat and food, and the climate of the locality in which it is reared. A prosciutto di Parma is paler and sweeter than, for instance, a prosciutto di montagna – mountain prosciutto. Secondly, salumi differ according to which cuts of meat are used, the proportion of fat to lean, the fineness of the mincing, the flavourings and the curing.

In what follows I describe some of the salumi that I like to serve as an antipasto. Together they form a dish called *affettato misto*, possibly the most common antipasto served in Italy. This dish of mixed cured meats is pretty to look at in its shades of pink and red, and one of the most appetising ways to start a meal.

You may be serving the *affettato* before a dish of pasta. (This is where I should point out that the word antipasto does *not* mean before the pasta. It means before the *'pasto'* – meal.) In Italy, however, *affettato* is often served as a *secondo* for lunch, not before but after the pasta which is de rigueur (only for lunch, though) in any self-respecting Italian family. Still, *primo* or *secondo*, *affettato misto* is an excellent dish, which, with some good bread or a piece of focaccia, followed by a lovely green salad and some cheese, is a perfect meal in its own right.

A good *affettato misto* should have a choice of at least five or six different meats. The following is a list of the products you can most easily find in this country. You can mix them to your liking, but one type of prosciutto and two types of salami should always be included. With a prosciutto I put two or three different kinds of salami: one from northern Italy, a Milano perhaps, which is mild and sweet, a peppery salame from the south and a Roman oval-shaped soppressata. An alternative that I like is a fennel-flavoured finocchiona, a salame from Tuscany. A few slices of the best mortadella, speckled with the acid green of fresh pistachio nuts, and of tasty coppa, which is a rolled, cured and boned shoulder of pork, would be just right for a good assortment.

The prosciutto can be prosciutto di Parma, the sweetest and palest of them all, or prosciutto di San Daniele, made in Friuli, of a darker red and stronger flavour. There is also a prosciutto di Carpegna, which is available in some of the best Italian delicatessens. I like it because it has a good flavour, is usually perfectly salted and contains the right amount of fat. A good prosciutto should always have some fat.

As for the quantity, I find that about 60g/2oz per person is enough. However, it is probably a good idea to buy more, because if you have a few slices left over they come in very handy for a sandwich the next day.

Try to buy your salumi from a delicatessen where it is sliced in front of you, rather than in vacuum packs from a supermarket. It is usually a better product and you can see with your own eyes if it is really the salumi it purports to be. For instance, proscutti have a mark of origin, their DOC, stamped on the skin. If you ask for the salumi to be sliced, remember that prosciutto should be sliced fine, but not so fine that you cannot transfer the slice to a dish without breaking it. Salami are better thicker, and the smaller the diameter of the salame, the thicker the cut should be.

CROSTINI E BRUSCHETTA

TOASTED AND GRILLED BREAD

Although I hate to think of food as being subject to fashion, I have to accept this fact of life. In this chapter you will find recipes for the most fashionable Italian antipasti of the early '90s. To me, however, Bruschetta and Crostini are dishes I have always made and shall always make, certainly not every week but at the right time of year, when I am in Italy or when I can get hold of the perfect tomatoes or am given a white truffle, or I am in the mood to make a loaf of bread (this latter a very rare event).

Crostini cover a broader range of dishes than Bruschetta. Crostini consist of slices of toasted bread moistened with olive oil on which different toppings are spread, while Bruschetta is either grilled country bread flavoured with olive oil and garlic, or the same grilled bread topped with tomato.

This antipasto has the advantage that it can be served as 'finger food' with the pre-prandial drinks, thus eliminating the washing-up of one set of plates.

FONDUTA PIEMONTESE

PIEDMONTESE FONDUE

Serves 4

400g/14oz Italian fontina
250ml/9fl oz full-fat milk
60g/2oz unsalted butter
4 egg yolks
1 white truffle or
1 tbsp truffle paste

Fontina, the best known cheese from Valle d'Aosta, used to be made at Mont Fontin, from which it takes its name. It is the main ingredient of this classic dish. The other characteristic ingredient is the white truffle of Alba. There are now various brands of truffle paste on the market, made with white truffles and porcini, which works very well in a fonduta. Sliced bread or crostini (see page 11) are served with fonduta for dipping into it. I also like to use thick slices of grilled polenta.

1 About 6 hours before you want to serve the fonduta, cut the fontina into small dices. Put in a bowl and add enough milk just to cover the cheese. Set aside.
2 Put the butter in the top of a double boiler, add the fontina with the milk and set over simmering water.
3 Cook, stirring constantly, for about 10 minutes until the cheese has melted, then beat in the egg yolks, one at a time. Continue cooking, beating the whole time, until the egg has been absorbed and the sauce reaches the consistency of double cream. If you are using truffle paste, mix it in at this point, off the heat.
4 Transfer the fonduta to individual soup dishes and slice the truffle over it, if you are using this food of the gods. Serve immediately.

CROSTINI ALLA TOSCANA
CHICKEN LIVER CROSTINI

In Tuscany, where this dish comes from, they add calf's melt (the spleen) to the chicken liver. Melt is added only to tone down the flavour of the liver and to give the mixture more volume. Of all offal, melt is the only one that is always used with other types of offal. To give this extra consistency to the mixture I have substituted minced beef for the melt. It works very well.

You can moisten the bread with vinsanto mixed with stock, instead of the more common olive oil. Vinsanto is a very strong wine from Chianti, made from grapes that are left to dry for several weeks before they are pressed.

Serves 6–8

225g/$\frac{1}{2}$lb chicken livers
4 tbsp olive oil (for cooking)
$\frac{1}{2}$ celery stick, very finely chopped
1 shallot, very finely chopped
2 small garlic cloves, chopped
3 tbsp chopped fresh parsley
100g/3$\frac{1}{2}$oz lean minced beef
1 tbsp tomato purée
6 tbsp dry white wine
salt and freshly ground black pepper
1 tbsp capers, rinsed and chopped
2 salted anchovies, boned and rinsed, or 4 canned anchovy fillets, chopped
30g/1oz unsalted butter

1 Remove the fat, gristle and any greenish bits from the chicken livers. Wash, dry and chop as finely as you can.
2 Put the olive oil in a saucepan and, when just hot, add the celery, shallot, garlic and parsley. Cook for 10 minutes until soft, stirring very frequently.
3 Add the chicken livers and the mince and cook very gently until the chicken livers have lost their raw colour and have become crumbly.
4 Mix in the tomato purée and cook for 1 minute. Raise the heat, pour over the wine and boil to reduce until nearly all the wine has evaporated. Lower the heat and add a little salt and plenty of pepper. Simmer gently for 30 minutes, adding a little hot water if the mixture gets too dry.
5 Mix in the capers and the anchovies. Add the butter and cook gently for 5 minutes, stirring constantly.
6 Spread the mixture on crostini (see page 11) moistened with olive oil or with a mixture of good meat stock and vinsanto.

PURE DI FAVE

BROAD BEAN PURÉE

Serves 6–8

1.35kg/3lb fresh broad beans,
or 450g/1lb frozen broad beans
salt and freshly ground
black pepper
3 garlic cloves, peeled
60g/2oz good-quality crustless
white bread
milk
90ml/3fl oz extra virgin olive oil

For this recipe you can use frozen broad beans which, although they do not have all the sweet mealiness of fresh ones, are picked and frozen at their best. Some recipes suggest using boiled potatoes instead of the bread. Either version is good.

1 Shell the broad beans, if you are using fresh ones. Cook the fresh or frozen beans in a saucepan of simmering water to which you have added 1 tbsp of salt and the garlic. The beans should cook at the lowest simmer. When the beans are tender, drain them and the garlic, reserving a cupful of the water. Allow to cool.

2 Put the bread in a bowl and pour in enough milk just to cover the bread.

3 Now you should have the patience to slip off the white skin from the beans. It's rather a boring and lengthy job, but it is necessary if you want a really creamy purée without those unpleasant pieces of papery skin. If there are any children around the house enlist their help; they usually love popping the beans out of their skin.

4 Put the broad beans, garlic and bread with its milk in a food processor and whizz to a purée, while gradually adding all but about 1 tbsp of the oil through the funnel. Taste and adjust the seasoning, adding a little of the reserved water if too thick.

5 You can spread the purée on crostini, (see page 11) moistened with the reserved oil, or serve the purée piled up in a dish surrounded by crostini, and let your guests or family do the work.

INTINGOLO DI PEPERONI E POMODORI SECCHI

—— RELISH OF PEPPERS AND SUN-DRIED TOMATOES ——

This colourful relish is good spooned over crostini (see page 11) or over slices of grilled polenta.

—————

1 Put the sun-dried tomatoes in a bowl. Add enough boiling water to cover, and the vinegar. Leave to soak for about 2 hours. Drain, reserving the liquid, and pat dry with kitchen paper towels. Cut the tomatoes into 1cm/½in pieces and set aside.

2 Heat the oven to 230°C/450°F/Gas Mark 8 and put a small baking tray in the oven.

3 Put the peppers on the tray and bake until they are soft, about 30 minutes. Remove from the oven and allow to cool a little.

4 Meanwhile, heat the onion and oil in a small frying pan. Sauté for a few minutes and then add the garlic, chilli and a little of the reserved tomato liquid, so that the *soffritto* (frying mixture) does not catch. Continue cooking until very soft, stirring frequently.

5 Peel the peppers, cut them in half and discard core and seeds. Cut them into 1cm/½in pieces and set aside.

6 Mix the tomato pieces into the *soffritto* in the pan, adding a little more of the tomato liquid if the mixture is dry. Cook, stirring frequently, for 5 minutes or so and then add the peppers. Let the peppers *insaporire* – take up the flavour.

7 Add the anchovy fillet to the pan and squash it down to a purée. Mix in the capers. Taste and adjust the seasoning. Serve warm or cold.

Serves 4

30g/1oz loose sun-dried tomatoes (not under oil)
2 tbsp red wine vinegar
2 large red and/or yellow peppers
½ sweet onion, very finely chopped
2 tbsp extra virgin olive oil
1 garlic clove, very finely chopped
½ dried chilli, crumbled
1 canned anchovy fillet, chopped
1 tbsp capers, rinsed and dried
salt and freshly ground black pepper

BRUSCHETTA

ROMAN GARLIC BREAD

Bruschetta is a crisp charred-tasting bread, originally from Rome (*bruscare* means 'to burn lightly' in Roman dialect). It is made with coarse country bread, which has a high nutritional value. For centuries bruschetta has been a staple dish of the poor, who ironically used to call it *cappone* – capon – since it was the nearest they could get to this delicacy of the rich. Nowadays bruschetta is served as an appetiser while you wait for your pasta to be ready. Bruschetta is also ideal to eat with fish soups.

Cut a loaf of coarse white bread – I use a Pugliese loaf – into really thick (1.5–2cm/$\frac{1}{2}$–$\frac{3}{4}$in) slices. For 6 slices you will need 2 squashed garlic cloves, some extra virgin olive oil, preferably a peppery Tuscan oil, and a good deal of freshly ground black pepper.

Score the slices lightly with the point of a small knife in a criss-cross fashion. Grill the bread on both sides over charcoal or wood embers (or under the grill) and then, while still hot, rub it with the garlic. Put the slices in a hot oven for 2 minutes, to make them crisp through, and then place them on a dish. Drizzle about 1 tbsp of oil over each one and sprinkle generously with pepper and a little salt.

This is the authentic, traditional bruschetta. In the last few years bruschetta has come to mean a thick, charred slice of bread moistened with olive oil and topped with tomatoes. Here is one recipe, made with sun-dried tomatoes for the winter.

BRUSCHETTA COI POMODORI SECCHI

BRUSCHETTA WITH SUN-DRIED TOMATOES

1 Reconstitute the sun-dried tomatoes at least 1 day in advance: put them in a bowl, cover them with boiling water, add the vinegar and leave to soak for 2 hours or so.

2 Drain the tomatoes and dry them thoroughly with kitchen paper towels. Cut them into 1cm/½in strips and put the strips in a deep dish. Pour over the olive oil, place the garlic here and there, and add the chilli. Leave to marinate for at least 24 hours.

3 Score the bread lightly with the point of a knife in a criss-cross fashion. Grill the slices on both sides and then moisten them with the oil in which the tomatoes have marinated. Lay a few strips of tomato over each slice of bread, leaving the garlic and chilli behind.

Serves 4–6

60g/2oz loose sun-dried
tomatoes (not under oil)
2 tbsp wine vinegar
6 tbsp extra virgin olive oil
3 garlic cloves, cut into
large pieces
2 dried chillies, cut in half
6 slices of good-quality
crusty bread

INSALATE

SALADS

A mixed antipasto for a large party, or an antipasto trolley in a restaurant, usually contains a number of different salads. Grilled peppers, for instance, are a classic antipasto salad, as are tomatoes with mozzarella and basil. The following five recipes include some of my favourites and some classics.

INSALATA DI PERE E FORMAGGIO
PEAR AND CHEESE SALAD

Serves 4

4 ripe William's or Comice pears
100g/3½oz Parmigiano
Reggiano or good
padano cheese
100g/3½oz mature pecorino
3 tbsp extra virgin olive oil
2 tbsp lemon juice
salt and freshly ground
black pepper
120g/4oz rocket

We have a saying in Italy, 'Do not let the peasant know how good pears are with cheese' – or he might pick all the pears off your tree! This salad is a sophisticated version of the classic pears with cheese.

1 Peel the pears, cut them into quarters and remove cores. Cut each quarter in half and pile them up in a deep dish.
2 Cut the cheeses into small cubes of about 1cm/½in. Mix into the pears.
3 Beat the oil and the lemon juice together and add salt and pepper to taste. Spoon about half this dressing over the pears and leave for 1 hour.
4 Surround the pear and cheese mound with rocket and dribble the rest of the dressing over it. Serve immediately.

INSALATA DI BROCCOLI CON LA MOLLICA

BROCCOLI AND BREADCRUMB SALAD

Brown breadcrumbs are better than white for this tasty dish from southern Italy. I make my soft crumbs in a food processor, a very quick job. You can use cauliflower instead of broccoli.

1 Divide the broccoli into small florets. Peel the outer layer from the stalks and cut them into small pieces. Blanch the florets and pieces of stalk in boiling salted water until just tender, about 5 minutes. Drain and dry with kitchen paper towels. Transfer to a bowl and add 2 tbsp of the oil. Toss gently, using two forks, rather than spoons, as they are less likely to break the florets.

2 Heat the rest of the oil in a frying pan and add the breadcrumbs. Cook for 3 minutes, stirring to coat them with the oil.

3 Chop all the other ingredients, except the olives, and add them to the bread mixture. Add the olives and cook for another minute or so, stirring well. Taste and add salt and pepper as necessary.

4 Toss half the breadcrumb mixture into the broccoli and spoon the rest over the top. Serve warm.

Serves 4

450g/1lb broccoli
6 tbsp extra virgin olive oil
125g/4oz fresh breadcrumbs
6 canned anchovy fillets, drained, or 3 salted anchovies, boned and rinsed
1 or 2 dried chillies, according to taste, seeded
2 garlic cloves, peeled
$1\frac{1}{2}$ tbsp capers, rinsed and dried
12 black olives, stoned and cut into strips
salt and freshly ground black pepper

PEPERONI ARROSTITI

GRILLED PEPPERS

Serves 4

4 beautiful red or yellow peppers
6 canned anchovy fillets,
drained, or 3 salted anchovies,
boned and rinsed
3 garlic cloves
2 tbsp chopped fresh parsley
1 small dried chilli, seeded
4 tbsp extra virgin olive oil

When peppers are grilled and skinned their taste is totally different from that of raw or sautéed peppers. To my mind they are much nicer, and they are certainly more digestible. You can prepare a few pounds of peppers when they are in season, and reasonably cheap, and keep them in the fridge in jars, well covered with olive oil, for 2 or 3 months.

When I serve these peppers on their own I like to dress them with the sauce given below, which is based on olive oil and garlic to which anchovy fillets and capers can be added. The sauce should be cooked for a couple of minutes so that the garlic and anchovy flavour combines well and becomes less pervasive. However, it is very important that the sauce should cook over very low heat or the garlic will burn and the anchovy become bitter.

1 Hold the peppers over the flame of a burner or set them in hot charcoal and grill them all over. (Alternatively, put them under the grill.) When the side in contact with the heat is charred, turn the pepper, until all the surface, including the top and bottom, is charred. As soon as all the skin is charred, take the pepper from the heat, otherwise the flesh will begin to burn and you will be left with paper-thin peppers.

2 Let the peppers cool and then remove the skin; it will come off very easily as long as the peppers have been well charred. Cut the peppers in half, remove the stalk and seeds and then cut them lengthwise into strips. Put them on a dish.

3 Pound the anchovies with the garlic, parsley and chilli in a mortar, or chop very finely.

4 Put the oil and the anchovy mixture in a very heavy pan and heat very slowly, stirring and pounding the whole time until the mixture is mashed. Spoon over the peppers and leave to marinate for at least 4 hours. The longer you leave them – up to a week – the better they get. Serve plenty of bread with them.

POMODORI CON LA MOZZARELLA E IL BASILICO

TOMATOES, MOZZARELLA AND BASIL

Serves 4

12 ripe tomatoes
salt and freshly ground
black pepper
350g/¾lb buffalo mozzarella
6 tbsp extra virgin olive oil
24 fresh basil leaves

This is the simplest and best summer antipasto. However, do not do it unless you have very good tomatoes – tasty and juicy, not woolly and dry. Sometimes you can buy the best round tomatoes from Calabria or Campania, sold still attached to their branches. Also, use buffalo mozzarella, which has a much deeper flavour than cows' milk mozzarella.

This might, in fact, be the sort of dish you can best do during your Mediterranean holidays, when you are sure of being able to buy the perfect ingredients.

1 The tomatoes must be peeled without being blanched, as this would soften them. To do this, use a swivel-action potato peeler. Make a small incision at one end of the tomato and start from there, working with the peeler by pushing it lightly backwards and forwards in a sawing movement. It is quite easy once you have learned the knack, which applies also to peeling raw peppers.
2 When all the tomatoes are peeled, cut them in half. Squeeze out a little of the seeds and juice, then sprinkle with salt. Lay the tomato halves on a wooden board, cut side down. Put the board in the fridge and leave for at least 30 minutes.
3 Wipe the inside of the tomatoes with kitchen paper towels and place them, cut side up, on a dish.
4 Cut the mozzarella into 24 slices or pieces. Put 1 piece inside each tomato half. Season with a generous grinding of pepper and drizzle with the olive oil.
5 Wipe the basil leaves with a moistened piece of kitchen paper towel. Place a leaf over each piece of mozzarella.

PANZANELLA

BREAD AND RAW VEGETABLE SALAD

A traditional rustic salad made in the summer with country bread and seasonal raw vegetables. Make it only when good tomatoes are in season, and with country-type bread. I recommend a Pugliese loaf, available in good supermarkets or in Italian delicatessens.

1 Cover the bread with cold water to which you have added 1 tbsp of the vinegar. Leave to soak until just soft, then squeeze out all the liquid and put the bread in a salad bowl. The bread should be damp but not wet. Break it up with a fork.

2 Add the basil, garlic, cucumber, onion and tomatoes. Season with salt and pepper. Toss thoroughly with the oil, using a fork to turn the mixture over. Chill for 30 minutes or so.

3 Taste and add more vinegar to your liking. It is not possible to specify the amount of vinegar, since it depends on its acidity and on personal taste.

Serves 4

8 slices of good-quality
white bread, 1 day old
about 2 tbsp wine vinegar
12 fresh basil leaves,
coarsely torn
$\frac{1}{2}$ garlic clove, finely chopped
$\frac{1}{2}$ cucumber, peeled and cut into
1cm/$\frac{1}{2}$in slices
$\frac{1}{2}$ red onion, very thinly sliced
225g/$\frac{1}{2}$lb ripe meaty tomatoes,
seeded and cut into
1cm/$\frac{1}{2}$in cubes
salt and freshly ground
black pepper
6 tbsp extra virgin olive oil

VERDURE RIPIENE

STUFFED VEGETABLES

One of the joys of walking round the old part of Genova is that you can still see shops selling farinata (chickpea tart), focaccia, pissaladeira and stuffed vegetables, all in the huge round copper pans in which they have been baked. Fat red tomatoes and shimmering red and yellow peppers fight for space with aubergines, of all colours from purple to ivory, and plump round courgettes, all soft and glistening with oil.

The recipes that follow are for my favourite stuffed vegetables. If you choose two or three of them and serve them together you are sure to give your family and friends one of the most appetising and satisfying antipasti ever.

The tomatoes, peppers and courgettes, for instance, go together very well, while the aubergines are perfect also by themselves. All these stuffed vegetables are best served warm or at room temperature, but not hot or chilled. They are even more delicious if made a day in advance.

FUNGHETTI RIPIENI ALLA GENOVESE

STUFFED MUSHROOM CAPS

Serves 4

20g/¾oz dried porcini
450g/1lb large-cap mushrooms
45g/1½oz fresh white
breadcrumbs
1 salted anchovy, boned and
rinsed, or 2 canned
anchovy fillets
1 or 2 garlic cloves, according
to taste, peeled
a handful of fresh marjoram
pinch of grated nutmeg
salt and freshly ground black
pepper
4 tbsp extra virgin olive oil
2 tbsp chopped fresh
flat-leaf parsley

If you can find them, use fresh porcini (ceps). Otherwise you can use cultivated large mushrooms, plus a little dried porcini for better flavour, as in this recipe.

1 Soak the dried porcini in a cupful of very hot water for 30 minutes. If necessary, rinse under cold water to remove any trace of grit. Dry thoroughly with kitchen paper towels.

2 Gently wipe the large-cap mushrooms with a damp cloth and detach the stalks.

3 Chop together the dried porcini, mushroom stalks, breadcrumbs, anchovies, garlic and marjoram. You can use a food processor, but do not reduce to pulp. Transfer to a bowl and add the nutmeg and salt and pepper to taste.

4 Heat the oven to 220°C/425°F/Gas Mark 7.

5 Heat 2 tbsp of the oil in a frying pan and add the mushroom and breadcrumb mixture. Sauté for 5 minutes, stirring frequently.

6 Lay the mushroom caps on an oiled baking tray, hollow side up. Sprinkle them with salt and then fill them with the crumb mixture. Sprinkle a pinch or two of parsley on top of each cap and then drizzle with the remaining oil. Bake for 10 to 15 minutes until the caps are soft. Serve at room temperature.

POMODORI AMMOLLICATI
TOMATOES STUFFED WITH BREADCRUMBS
AND PARSLEY

1 Cut the tomatoes in half. Remove the seeds and sprinkle with salt. Lay them cut side down on a wooden board to drain for about 30 minutes. Wipe the inside of each half with kitchen paper towels.

2 Heat the oven to 180°C/350°F/Gas Mark 4.

3 Put the parsley, garlic, capers, chilli, breadcrumbs and oregano in a bowl. Mix well and then add 4 tbsp of the oil. Season with a little salt and some pepper. Mix well to a paste.

4 Oil the bottom of a shallow baking dish or roasting tin. Place the tomatoes in the dish, cut side up.

5 Spoon a little of the breadcrumb mixture into each half tomato and then drizzle with the rest of the oil. Bake for about 30 minutes until the tomatoes are soft but still whole. Serve at room temperature.

Serves 3 or 4

6 large round tomatoes, ripe but firm
salt and freshly ground black pepper
2 tbsp chopped fresh flat-leaf parsley
2 garlic cloves, finely chopped
1 tbsp capers, rinsed and chopped
$\frac{1}{2}$ small dried chilli, chopped
4 tbsp dried white breadcrumbs
$\frac{1}{2}$ tbsp dried oregano
5 tbsp extra virgin olive oil

MELANZANE RIPIENE

AUBERGINE STUFFED WITH SAUSAGE, PINE NUTS AND CURRANTS

Serves 4

2 aubergines, weighing about 450g/1lb each
salt and freshly ground black pepper
4 tbsp extra virgin olive oil
1 large garlic clove, finely chopped
$\frac{1}{2}$ small onion or 1 shallot, very finely chopped
$\frac{1}{2}$ celery stick, very finely chopped
225g/$\frac{1}{2}$lb spicy luganega or other spicy coarse-grained pure pork continental sausage, skinned and crumbled
30g/1oz soft white breadcrumbs
3 tbsp pine nuts
2 tbsp capers, rinsed and dried
1 egg
1 tbsp dried oregano
3 tbsp freshly grated pecorino or Parmesan
3 tbsp dried currants
1 large ripe tomato

1 Wash and dry the aubergines. Cut them in half lengthways and scoop out all the flesh with the help of a small sharp knife and then with a small teaspoon, leaving just enough pulp to cover the skin. Be careful not to pierce the skin.

2 Chop the pulp of the aubergine coarsely and place in a colander. Sprinkle with salt, mix well and leave to drain for about 1 hour.

3 Put 3 tbsp of the oil, the garlic, onion and celery in a frying pan and sauté over low heat until soft, stirring frequently. Add the sausage and cook for 20 minutes, turning it over frequently.

4 Meanwhile, squeeze the liquid from the chopped aubergine pulp and dry thoroughly with kitchen paper towels. Add the aubergine pulp to the pan and fry gently for a few minutes, stirring frequently. Taste and adjust the seasoning.

5 Heat the oven to 190°C/375°F/Gas Mark 5.

6 Add the breadcrumbs to the mixture in the frying pan. After 2–3 minutes, mix in the pine nuts. Cook for a further 30 seconds, then transfer to a bowl.

7 Add the capers, egg, oregano, cheese, currants and pepper to taste to the mixture in the bowl and mix very thoroughly. Taste and add salt if necessary.

8 Pat dry the inside of the aubergine shells. Oil a baking dish large enough to hold the aubergine shells in a single layer. Place the aubergine shells, one next to the other, in the dish and fill them with the sausage mixture.

9 Cut the tomato into strips and place 2 or 3 strips on the top of each aubergine half. Drizzle with the rest of the oil. Add 120ml/ 4fl oz of water to the bottom of the dish. Cover the dish tightly with foil and bake for 20 minutes. Remove the foil and bake for a further 20 minutes.

This dish is best eaten warm, an hour or so after it comes out of the oven.

PEPERONI AMMOLLICATI

PEPPERS STUFFED WITH BREADCRUMBS

AND PARSLEY

Serves 4

700g/1½lb red and
yellow peppers
5 tbsp extra virgin olive oil
salt and freshly ground
black pepper
3 tbsp chopped fresh
flat-leaf parsley
2 garlic cloves, finely chopped
1 tbsp capers, rinsed and
chopped
½ small dried chilli, chopped
2 salted anchovies, boned,
rinsed and chopped
4 tbsp dried white breadcrumbs

The stuffing for peppers is basically the same as that for tomatoes. I prefer, however, to omit the oregano and to add salted anchovies. Use red and yellow peppers, but not green because they are not sweet enough.

1 Cut the peppers into quarters and remove the cores, ribs and seeds. Heat 4 tbsp of the oil in a large frying pan until very hot and then add the peppers, skin side down. Sprinkle with salt and pepper and cook for about 10 minutes, shaking the pan occasionally.

2 Heat the oven to 180°C/350°F/Gas Mark 4.

3 Mix together the remaining ingredients in a bowl.

4 When the peppers are just soft, place them in an oiled baking dish, cut side up. Pour the juices from the pan into the breadcrumb mixture and mix well. Taste and check seasoning.

5 Place a small mound of stuffing into each piece of pepper, drizzle with the remaining oil and bake for 15 minutes.

ZUCCHINE AL FORNO
BAKED COURGETTES WITH MINT
AND GARLIC STUFFING

1 Cut the courgettes in half lengthways. Make some diagonal incisions on the cut side. Sprinkle the cut side lightly with salt and place the courgette halves on a wooden board, cut side down. This will allow some of the liquid to drain away.

2 Heat the oven to 180°C/350°F/Gas Mark 4.

3 Put the chopped herbs in a bowl and add the garlic and breadcrumbs. Add half the oil gradually, while beating with a fork. Season with a good grinding of pepper and with very little salt.

4 Oil a shallow baking dish or a lasagne dish large enough to hold all the courgette halves in a single layer.

5 Wipe the courgettes with kitchen paper towels and lay them in the dish, cut side up. Spoon a little of the herb mixture over each half. Drizzle 1 tbsp of the oil over the halves and cover the dish with foil. Bake for 15 minutes. Remove the foil and continue baking until the courgettes are tender and the top is crisp, about 10 minutes longer.

6 Drizzle with the remaining oil while the courgettes are still hot. Serve warm or at room temperature.

Serves 4

450g/1lb medium courgettes
salt and freshly ground
black pepper
2 tbsp chopped parsley
4 tbsp chopped fresh mint
2 garlic cloves, chopped
4 tbsp dried breadcrumbs
6 tbsp extra virgin olive oil

ANTIPASTI DI PESCE E CARNE

———— FISH AND MEAT ANTIPASTI ————

The following recipes are for dishes whose main ingredient, whether fish or meat, is usually served as a main course. In these recipes the fish and meat is prepared in a light and lively way that is extremely appetising and therefore particularly suited to an antipasto.

COZZE RIPIENE

STUFFED MUSSELS

Serves 4

900g/2lb mussels
2 unwaxed lemons, cut into quarters
6 garlic cloves, peeled
120ml/4fl oz extra virgin olive oil
5 tbsp chopped fresh parsley
5 tbsp dried breadcrumbs
salt and freshly ground black pepper

This is the basic recipe for cozze ripiene, to which other ingredients such as grated pecorino, tomato sauce, capers and so on can be added.

1 Mussels are much cleaner these days, because they are usually farmed. However, they still need a good cleaning. Put them in a sink full of cold water and scrub them with a stiff brush. Scrape off any barnacles and beards. Discard any mussel that stays open after tapping it against a hard surface: it is dead. Rinse the mussels in several changes of water until the water is clean, and no sand is left at the bottom of the sink.

2 Put the lemon quarters and 5 cloves of garlic in a large frying pan. Add the mussels, cover and cook over high heat until the mussels are open. Shake the pan occasionally. (Discard any that remain closed. They might be full of sand.)

3 Heat the oven to 220°C/425°F/Gas Mark 7.

4 Remove the top of each shell. Loosen the mussels in the bottom shell and place them on a baking tray.

5 Filter the mussel liquid left in the pan through a sieve lined with muslin into a bowl. Mix in the oil, parsley, breadcrumbs, and salt and pepper to taste. Finely chop the remaining garlic and add to the mixture.

6 Place a little of the parsley and breadcrumb mixture over each mussel and bake for about 7 minutes until golden brown.

INSALATA CALDA DI MARE
— WARM SEAFOOD SALAD —

This is a very popular antipasto, and every region, every town, even every cook has a slightly different version. You can vary the fish you use, according to your taste and the availability of the fish in the market. Remember to have a good selection of textures, but do not use any kind of blue fish, as its taste would be too strong.

Here is my seafood salad, which I like to serve warm.

1 Put the mussels in a sink full of cold water and scrub them with a stiff brush, scraping off any barnacles and beards with a small knife. Discard any open mussel that fails to close after being tapped hard on a hard surface. Rinse the mussels in several changes of water until the water is clean and no sand is left at the bottom of the sink.

2 Put the mussels in a large saucepan, cover and cook over high heat until they are open, shaking the pan every now and then. (Discard any mussels that remain closed.) Shell the mussels and put the meat in a bowl; discard the shells. Filter the mussel liquid left in the pan through a sieve lined with muslin. Pour the liquid over the mussels. Add the chilli for flavouring.

3 Ask your fishmonger to clean and skin the squid. If he is not prepared to do it, proceed as follows. Hold the sac in one hand and pull off the tentacles with the other hand. The contents of the sac will come out too. Cut the tentacles above the eyes. Squeeze out the thin bony beak in the centre of the tentacles. Peel off the skin from the sac and the flap. Remove the translucent backbone from inside the sac and rinse the sac and tentacles under cold water. Cut the sac into strips and the tentacles into bite-size pieces.

Serves 6

450g/1lb mussels
1 dried chilli
450g/1lb squid
4 tbsp wine vinegar
1 onion, cut in half
2 bayleaves
salt and freshly ground black pepper
350g/¾lb monkfish
225g/½lb shelled scallops
12 large raw prawns in shell, about 225g/½lb
1 garlic clove, finely chopped
3 tbsp chopped fresh flat-leaf parsley
3 tbsp lemon juice
150ml/¼ pint extra virgin olive oil
black olives to garnish

4 Put about 1.5 litres/$2\frac{1}{2}$ pints of cold water in a saucepan, add 2 tbsp of the vinegar, the onion, 1 bayleaf and some salt and bring to the boil. Add the squid and cook over a steady simmer for 5 to 15 minutes, depending on their size. Squid are cooked when they become white and lose their translucency and you can pierce them with a fork. Remove the squid from the water with a slotted spoon, drain well and add to the mussels in the bowl.

5 Cut the monkfish into large chunks and add to the boiling water in which the squid have cooked. Simmer gently for about 2 minutes. Remove from the heat, leaving the fish in the liquid.

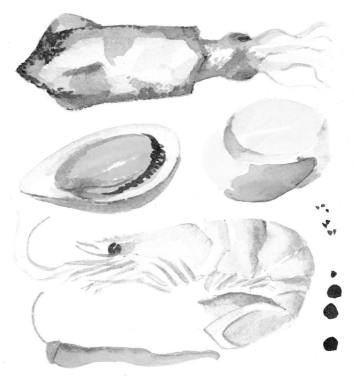

6 While the monkfish is cooking, put another saucepan on the heat with about 600ml/1 pint of hot water, the remaining bayleaf, the rest of the vinegar and some salt. When the water is boiling, add the scallops. Simmer for 2 minutes after the water has returned to the boil and then remove with a slotted spoon. If scallops are large, cut them into quarters. Add to the bowl containing the mussels and squid.

7 Put the prawns into the boiling water in which the scallops have cooked. Simmer for 1 minute after the water has come back to the boil. Drain and set aside to cool.

8 Drain the monkfish. Remove any bone and skin and cut into bite-size pieces. Add the fish to the bowl with the other seafood.

9 Peel the prawns and, if necessary, devein them. Choose about half a dozen of the largest prawns and set aside for garnish. Cut the other prawns into rounds and add to the bowl.

10 Prepare the sauce: mix the garlic, parsley and lemon juice together in a small bowl. Add a generous grinding of black pepper and some salt. Beat in the oil slowly. Taste and adjust seasonings.

11 Before serving, put the bowl containing the seafood over a saucepan of simmering water. Cover the bowl and heat until the fish is warm, not hot. Stir it once or twice, using a fork, not a spoon, which would tend to break the pieces of fish.

12 Fish the chilli out of the bowl and discard it. Spoon the sauce over the seafood and toss gently but thoroughly. Pile the seafood salad in a deep dish and garnish with the reserved prawns and the olives.

MAGRONI DI ANATRA ALL'ACETO BALSAMICO SUL LETTO DI VALERIANELLA

DUCK BREASTS WITH BALSAMIC VINEGAR ON A BED OF LAMB'S LETTUCE

Serves 6

2 duck breasts (magrets), about 350g/¾lb each
salt and freshly ground black pepper
2–3 tbsp balsamic vinegar, according to taste and acidity
225g/½lb lamb's lettuce
3 tbsp extra virgin olive oil

French duck breasts, called magrets de canard, are now on the market; these are the breasts of the larger but leaner Barbary ducks. These breasts have less fat under the skin, and they are ideal for this type of quick cooking. Balsamic vinegar is a superb condiment for duck. The sauce it produces when mixed with the cooking juices is rich in flavour and yet tangy enough to cut across the richness of the meat. The lamb's lettuce adds lemony crispness and a fresh look. If you cannot find lamb's lettuce, use curly endive, cut into thin strips.

1 Score the skin of the duck breasts with the point of a small sharp knife. Rub with salt and pepper.

2 Heat a frying pan. Place the breasts in the pan, skin side down, and cook over moderate heat for 7 to 9 minutes, depending on thickness. The fat will run out. Pour out nearly all the fat (keep it for sauté potatoes).

3 Spoon 1 tbsp of balsamic vinegar over the breasts and turn them over. Cook for 2 minutes on the underside. Lift out the breasts and place on a board. Carve across into 5mm/¼in slices. Place the slices on a warm dish. Cover with foil and leave for 10 minutes, for the muscle to relax.

4 Add the remaining balsamic vinegar and about 4 tbsp of hot water to the frying pan and stir well to deglaze the juices. Taste to see if you need a little more vinegar and/or a little more water.

5 Toss the lamb's lettuce with the oil and season with a little salt and a generous grinding of pepper. Make a bed of lamb's lettuce on each plate.

6 Place the duck slices on the lamb's lettuce and pour over the juices from the pan. Do not wait too long to serve the dish after you have poured the juices or the lettuce will 'tire' too much.

SARDE A BECCAFICU
STUFFED SARDINES

The combination of sardines and orange is to be found only in Sicily, and this dish produces the best of this unusual yet delicious mixture of flavours. It is an antipasto that is very popular in Palermo and Messina, a peasant dish whose name derives from its appearance. The boned sardines are rolled up around a spoonful of stuffing and set in a dish with their tails in the air, making them look like fat little *beccafichi* – warblers – pecking at the dish.

---

1 Few fishmongers are willing to prepare the sardines for you, so this is what you should do. Cut off the heads and the fins (but not the tail), slit the belly and clean out the insides. Lay the sardines on a board, open side down, and press the backbone down gently. Cut the backbone at the tail end and remove it. Wash and dry the fish.

2 Put the currants in a bowl and cover with boiling water. Leave them to plump up for 5 to 10 minutes. Drain and dry them thoroughly with kitchen paper towels.

3 Heat 3 tbsp of the oil in a frying pan and fry the breadcrumbs until nicely brown. Mix in the pine nuts, garlic, parsley and

Serves 6

900g/2lb fresh sardines
4 level tbsp dried currants
5 tbsp olive oil
75g/2½oz dried white
breadcrumbs
4 level tbsp pine nuts
1 garlic clove, finely chopped
2 level tbsp chopped fresh
flat-leaf parsley
2 level tbsp grated
mature pecorino
salt and freshly ground
black pepper
12 bayleaves
juice of 1 orange
juice of ½ lemon
1 tsp sugar

currants. Sauté gently for a few minutes and then remove the pan from the heat. Add the cheese and pepper to taste. Taste and add salt if necessary.

4 Heat the oven to 180°C/350°F/Gas Mark 4.

5 Sprinkle the sardines on both sides with a little salt and pepper and place them skin side down. Spread a generous teaspoonful of stuffing over each fish and roll up towards the tail. Place them in an oiled baking dish with the tails sticking up in the air.

6 Stick the bayleaves here and there among the little bundles. Drizzle the orange and lemon juices and the rest of the oil all over. Sprinkle with the sugar.

7 Place the dish in the oven and bake for 15 minutes or so. Serve at room temperature.

SFOGI IN SAOR

SOLE FILLETS IN A SWEET-AND-SOUR SAUCE

Serves 6–8

flour
salt
oil for deep frying
700g/1½lb sole fillets
60g/2oz sultanas
2 tbsp olive oil
225g/½lb sweet onions,
thinly sliced
2 tsp sugar
120ml/4fl oz good wine vinegar
4 bayleaves
60g/2oz pine nuts
2–3 pinches of ground cinnamon
2 cloves
12 black peppercorns,
lightly bruised

The taste of this sauce, in which the sole is marinated for 2 days, is strongly reminiscent of Middle Eastern cooking. This is understandable, as this is a dish from Venice, a city which in the past had important trade links with the Orient.

Sfogi in saor (Venetian dialect for *'sogliole in sapore'*, meaning sole in a sauce) is one of the dishes traditionally eaten in Venice during the Feast of the Redeemer, which falls on the third Sunday in July, when the lagoon is lit by thousands of fireworks and carpeted with boats of every size.

1 Spread some flour on a board and season with salt.

2 Heat oil for deep frying in a wok or a frying pan. Meanwhile, coat the fish lightly in the flour.

3 When the oil is very hot but not smoking (test by frying a small piece of bread: it should brown in 50 seconds), slide in the sole fillets, a few at a time. Fry gently for about 3 minutes on each side until a golden crust has formed. With a fish slice, transfer the fish to a plate lined with kitchen paper towels to drain.

4 Soak the sultanas in a little warm water to plump them.

5 Heat the olive oil and onions in a small frying pan. Add a pinch of salt and the sugar. Cook the onions gently, stirring frequently, until golden. Turn the heat up and pour in the wine vinegar. Boil briskly until the liquid is reduced by half.

6 Lay the fish neatly in a shallow dish. Pour over the onion sauce and put the bayleaves on top. Drain the sultanas and scatter them on top of the dish together with the pine nuts, spices and peppercorns. Cover the dish with cling film and leave to marinate for 24 hours.

If you want to keep the dish for 2 days or more, refrigerate it. Take the dish out of the fridge at least 2 or 3 hours before you want to serve it, so that it has time to reach room temperature.

IL MIO CARPACCIO

MY CARPACCIO

Created by Giuseppe Cipriani at Harry's Bar for one of his clients who was on a strict diet, Carpaccio has now become the byword for any fish or meat (alas, even chicken) served raw and dressed with some sort of olive-oil-based sauce. Each cook varies the sauce according to his or her preference, so you can experiment with your Carpaccio. This is my version.

I have found it very difficult to slice the beef thinly without an electric carving knife.

Serves 4

350g/¾lb fillet of beef
1 egg yolk
180ml/6fl oz extra virgin olive oil
3 tbsp lemon juice
1 tsp Dijon mustard
a few drops of Tabasco sauce
salt and freshly ground black pepper

1 Put the beef in the freezer for about 3 hours to harden it; this makes it easier to slice thinly.
2 Put the egg yolk in a food processor with 2 tbsp of the oil, the lemon juice, mustard, Tabasco, and some salt and pepper and process for 30 seconds.
3 Add the rest of the oil slowly through the hole in the lid. The sauce will become like a thin mayonnaise. Taste and adjust the seasoning.
4 Remove the beef from the freezer and place on a board. Using an electric carving knife, or a *very* sharp knife, slice it very thinly. Allow the meat to come back to room temperature – about 1 hour.
5 Place the meat neatly on a dish and pour the sauce over it before serving.

OTHER FAVOURITES

The title of this section is self-explanatory. These are recipes I wanted to include, but which did not fit into any of the other categories.

RADICCHIO ROSSO E CICORIA BELGA ALLA TREVISANA

GRILLED RADICCHIO AND CHICORY

Serves 6

450g/1lb red radicchio
225g/½lb chicory
6 tbsp extra virgin olive oil
salt and freshly ground
black pepper

The radicchio rosso used in Veneto for this dish is the long radicchio of Treviso, which can now sometimes be found in specialist greengrocers during the autumn. It has the characteristic bitterness of radicchio, delicate yet more pronounced than the round Rosa di Chioggia, which is the kind of radicchio available everywhere all year round. The Rosa di Chioggia is a modern type of radicchio which is grown in greenhouses. It is tougher in texture and blander in flavour, with a similarity to white cabbage. However, the use of heat in this recipe brings out the flavour. Chicory is very good prepared in this way.

1 Preheat the grill.
2 Wash the radicchio and chicory carefully. Dry thoroughly. Cut the radicchio into quarters and the chicory in half, both lengthwise.
3 Place the radicchio and chicory in the grill pan (or on a hot griddle). Spoon over the oil and season with salt and a generous amount of pepper.
4 Cook under the grill (or on the griddle) for 10 minutes, taking care to turn the heat down if the vegetables start to burn. Turn the pieces over half-way through the cooking. The vegetables are ready when the thick core can be pierced easily.
5 Transfer the grilled vegetables to a dish and spoon over the juice from the grill pan. Serve hot or cold.

CIPOLLINE BRASATE
BRAISED BABY ONIONS

These onions, served cold, often form part of a spectacular Piedmontese antipasto. They can also accompany cold meat or, served hot, boiled or braised meat dishes. The onions used in Italy are the white, squat kind, very sweet in taste. Unfortunately they are not easily available outside Italy, but you can use small young pickling onions instead.

Serves 4

700g/1½lb small onions
4 tbsp olive oil
15g/½oz butter
2 tsp tomato purée dissolved in
150ml/¼ pint hot water
2 tbsp sugar
2 tbsp red wine vinegar
salt and freshly ground
black pepper

1 Put the onions in a pan of boiling water. Bring back to the boil and blanch for 1 minute. Drain and remove the outside skin, taking care to remove only the dangling roots and not the base of the root, otherwise the onions will come apart during the cooking.
2 Choose a large sauté pan and put in the onions, olive oil and butter. Sauté the onions until golden, shaking the pan often.
3 Add the diluted tomato purée, sugar, vinegar, and salt and pepper to taste. Cook, uncovered, for about 1 hour, adding a little more water if necessary. The onions are ready when they are a rich brown colour and can easily be pierced by a fork. Serve hot or cold, but not chilled.

FRITTELLE DI MOZZARELLA

MOZZARELLA AND PARMESAN FRITTERS

Serves 4

225g/½lb Italian mozzarella
1 size-2 egg
75g/2½oz Parmesan,
freshly grated
2 tbsp flour
12 fresh basil leaves
1 small garlic clove,
finely chopped
salt and freshly ground
black pepper
oil for deep frying

The mozzarella must be left out of its pack for 24 hours to allow it to dry out.

1 Grate the mozzarella through the largest holes of a cheese grater and put it in a bowl.
2 Beat the egg lightly and add to the bowl with the Parmesan and flour.
3 Wipe the basil leaves with damp kitchen paper towels and snip them with scissors. Mix into the mozzarella mixture with the garlic, a generous grinding of pepper and a little salt. (Add salt with caution because the Parmesan is salty). Mix thoroughly.
4 With damp hands, shape the mixture into small balls, the size of a walnut. If the mixture is too sloppy add a little more flour. Put the balls on a wooden board and chill for at least 30 minutes.
5 Heat oil in a wok or a small deep saucepan. When the oil is very hot but not yet smoking (the right temperature is 180°C/350°F, i.e. when a small piece of bread will turn golden in 50 seconds) slide in the cheese balls. Do not crowd the pan or they will not fry properly. Turn them over and when they are deep gold all over, fish them out with a slotted spoon and put them on kitchen paper towels to drain. Serve hot.

CAROTE IN AGRODOLCE

CARROTS IN A WINE AND HERB

—————————————— SAUCE ——————————————

Serves 6

900g/2lb carrots
6 tbsp olive oil
250ml/9fl oz dry white wine
120ml/4fl oz white wine vinegar
2 sprigs of fresh flat-leaf parsley
2 sprigs of fresh thyme
4 fresh sage leaves
2 bayleaves
4 sprigs of fresh mint
2 garlic cloves, cut in half
salt and freshly ground
black pepper
2 tbsp sugar

Vegetables these days badly need an uplift. This agrodolce treatment is just the thing to bring out the delicious sweet taste of the carrots.

————————————

1 Cut the carrots into thick matchsticks and put them in a sauté pan.

2 Add all the other ingredients plus 250ml/9fl oz of water. Bring to the boil and cook, uncovered, for 30 minutes. The carrots will still be quite crunchy.

3 Lift the carrots out of the pan with a slotted spoon and put them in a bowl.

4 Boil the liquid rapidly to reduce until it is very tasty and of a beautiful deep gold colour. Most of the water will have evaporated and you will be left with a delicious hot herby vinaigrette. Taste and adjust the seasoning.

5 Pour the reduced liquid over the carrots and leave to marinate for 48 hours.

6 Remove the herbs and garlic before serving.

UOVA SODA ALLA PUGLIESE CON I POMODORI SECCHI

HARD-BOILED EGGS WITH PARSLEY AND BREADCRUMB
TOPPING AND SUN-DRIED TOMATOES

Serves 4

120g/4oz loose sun-dried
tomatoes (not under oil)
6 tbsp good red wine vinegar,
but not balsamic vinegar
150ml/¼ pint extra virgin olive oil
salt and freshly ground
black pepper
6 eggs
6 tbsp dried white breadcrumbs
3 garlic cloves, chopped
6 tbsp chopped fresh
flat-leaf parsley
2–3 dried chillies, according to
taste, chopped

These eggs are served at room temperature. I like to surround them with charred and peeled yellow and red peppers (page 22), or, as here, with sun-dried tomatoes generously dressed with extra virgin olive oil and seasoned with garlic, salt and pepper. I also scatter black olives here and there round the dish.

1 Put the sun-dried tomatoes in a bowl and cover with boiling water. Add 4 tbsp of the vinegar and leave to soak for about 2 hours. Lift the tomatoes out of the liquid and pat dry thoroughly with kitchen paper towels. Drizzle 2 tbsp of the oil over the tomatoes, season with salt and pepper and set aside while you prepare the eggs.

2 Hard-boil the eggs: lower them into a pan of simmering water and cook for 8 minutes, no longer, so that the yolks will be just hard. Put the saucepan under cold running water and leave for 1 minute. Crack the shells all round and peel them off. Leave the eggs to cool right through in the cold water while you make the topping.

3 Heat half the remaining oil in a small frying pan. Add the breadcrumbs and sauté for a couple of minutes, stirring constantly, until the crumbs are golden. Put aside 2–3 tbsp of the remaining oil. Add the rest of the oil to the pan with the remaining vinegar and all the other ingredients. Sauté gently for a further couple of minutes. Taste and adjust the seasoning.

4 Drain and dry the eggs. Cut them in half lengthways. To prevent the egg halves sliding on the dish, slice off a tiny bit of the white on the round side, to give a flat base. Arrange the eggs on a

serving dish and drizzle with the reserved oil. Season lightly with salt and pepper and pile about 2 tsp of the topping over each egg half. Surround with the tomatoes.

CAPONATA

AUBERGINE, ONION AND CELERY STEW

Thanks to the creativity of the Sicilians, the humble aubergine here forms the basis of one of the grandest vegetable dishes. Caponata appears in many different versions throughout the island. The dish can be garnished with tiny boiled octopus, with a small lobster, with prawns or with *bottarga* – the dried roe of the grey mullet or of the tunny fish, a speciality of Siciliy and Sardinia. I garnish this one with hard-boiled eggs, thus making it a perfect vegetarian dish.

The secret of a good caponata is that the three vegetables, aubergine, celery and onion, must be cooked separately and only after cooking combined together and added to the other ingredients. Caponata is best made at least 24 hours in advance.

1 Cut the aubergines into 1cm/½in cubes.

2 Heat 2.5cm/1in of vegetable oil in a frying pan. When the oil is hot (it is ready when it sizzles around a cube of aubergine) add a layer of aubergines and fry until golden brown on all sides. Drain on kitchen paper towels. Repeat until all the aubergines are cooked. Season each batch lightly with salt.

3 Cut the celery into pieces of the same size as the aubergine. Fry it in the oil in which you fried the aubergine, until golden and crisp. Drain it on kitchen paper towels.

Serves 4

700g/1½lb aubergines
vegetable oil for frying
salt and freshly ground
black pepper
the inner sticks of 1 celery head,
coarse threads removed
100ml/3½fl oz olive oil
1 onion, very finely sliced
225g/8oz Italian canned
plum tomatoes, chopped
1 tbsp sugar
90ml/3fl oz white wine vinegar
1 tbsp grated bitter chocolate
60g/2oz capers
60g/2oz large green olives,
stoned and quartered
2 hard-boiled eggs

4 Pour the olive oil into a clean frying pan and add the onion. Sauté gently for about 10 minutes until soft. Add the tomatoes and cook, stirring frequently, over moderate heat for about 15 minutes. Season with salt and pepper.

5 While the sauce is cooking, heat the sugar and vinegar in a small saucepan. Add the chocolate, capers and olives and cook gently until the chocolate has melted. Add to the tomato sauce and cook for 5 further minutes.

6 Mix the aubergines and celery into the tomato sauce. Stir and cook for 20 minutes so that the flavours of the ingredients can blend together. Pour the caponata into a serving dish and allow to cool.

7 Pass the hard-boiled eggs through the smallest holes of a food mill, or push through a metal sieve. Before serving, cover the caponata with the sieved eggs.

BAGNA CAODA
HOT GARLICKY DIP FOR RAW VEGETABLES

Bagna caôda is a peasant dish from Piedmont, where, in country kitchens, it is made in earthenware pots kept hot on glowing embers. An earthenware pot, small and deep, is indeed by far the best receptacle in which to make it. You will also need a table heater or a candle burner in the middle of the table to keep the bagna caôda hot, though it must not cook. The vegetables are dipped, raw, into the sauce, although some cooks prefer to blanch the cardoons and the celeriac.

Plenty of crusty bread and full-bodied red wine, such as a Dolcetto, Barolo or Nebbiolo, are the other essentials. The oil used should be a mild extra virgin one from Liguria, not a peppery oil from Tuscany.

Serves 4–6

an assortment of raw vegetables such as cardoons, celery, cauliflower, courgettes, carrots, radishes and peppers
75g/2½oz butter
5 garlic cloves, very finely sliced or chopped
60g/2oz salted anchovies, boned, rinsed and chopped, or canned anchovy fillets, chopped
150ml/¼ pint extra virgin olive oil
salt

1 First prepare the vegetables. Cardoons are the traditional vegetable for bagna caôda, but they are not easy to find in this country. If you find some, they will usually have already had their outer leaves and tough stalks removed. You will have to remove the strings, as you do with celery sticks. Cut the stalks and the heart into suitable pieces. Rub any cut part with lemon to prevent discolouring. Prepare all the other vegetables as you do for a normal dip, i.e. washing, scraping, stringing, according to the vegetable, and then cutting into fingers. Choose the best specimens and discard any bruised parts.

2 Melt the butter in a small, deep earthenware pot or a very heavy-based saucepan over the lowest simmer. As soon as the butter has melted and has begun to foam, add the garlic and cook for a minute or so. The garlic should not colour.

3 Add the anchovies to the pot and pour in the oil very gradually, stirring the whole time. Cook for about 10 minutes, always on the lowest possible heat and stirring constantly. The sauce should never come near to boiling point. The dip is ready when the anchovies have become a paste. Taste and add salt if necessary. Pepper is not added to traditional bagna caôda.

4 Bring the pot to the table together with the prepared vegetables, and place it over a low flame or on a table heater.

La Pasta

'I like all simple things, boiled eggs, oysters
and caviare, *truite au bleu*, grilled salmon,
roast lamb (the saddle by preference),
cold grouse, treacle tart and rice pudding.
But of all simple things the only one I can eat
day in and day out, not only without disgust
but with the eagerness of an appetite
unimpaired by excess, is macaroni.'

From a short story, *The Hairless Mexican*
by W Somerset Maugham

INTRODUCTION

Pasta is the simplest food, even simpler than bread, consisting only of semolina and water for dried pasta and flour and eggs for home-made pasta. It is also the food that can change its character and appearance more than any other, like some great character-actor, assuming countless different roles. Think of the golden lightness of a delicate dish of tagliatelle with butter and compare it with the intriguing, exotic flavour of a green dish of spaghetti with pesto, or the rich earthiness of a dish of baked lasagne. All are equally good in their different ways, and pasta is the main ingredient of them all.

TYPES OF PASTA

We Italians never look down on dried pasta. We consider it ideal for many sauces and would never regard it as merely a substitute for home-made pasta.

Factory-made **dried pasta** is made from durum wheat ground into semolina and mixed to a paste with water. The dough is forced through perforated metal discs to form the desired shape of pasta, and then dried. It should be buff-yellow, translucent and slightly shiny. The most common kinds of dried pasta are spaghetti, long pasta of various widths and lengths, shapes such as fusilli, conchiglie and penne, lasagne and small pasta for soups.

The '**fresh pasta**' sold in delicatessens or supermarkets is made with durum wheat semolina, flour, eggs and water. Though it is convenient, it certainly is not as good as home-made pasta, and it compares badly with dried pasta of a good Italian brand.

Home-made pasta has a lightness and delicacy that shop-bought 'fresh pasta' cannot match. So, when you want to make a recipe that calls for fresh pasta, do try to make it yourself, whether by hand or with the help of a machine. Remember, though, that it is not easy to make pasta by hand without practice, time and a long, thin pasta rolling pin.

Luckily there are good machines to speed up the task. Some electric machines make good pasta, but they are expensive, noisy and difficult to clean. The hand-cranked machines are cheap and easily obtained.

THE COOKING OF PASTA

The time pasta takes to cook differs according to its quality and shape, whether it is fresh or dried, and, of course, personal preference. Even in Italy a plate of spaghetti that would be perfect in Naples might be considered undercooked in Milan. So I suggest you follow the table as a working guide.

COOKING TIMES FOR PASTA

Cooking time is calculated after the water returns to the boil

HOME-MADE PASTA	FRESH	DRIED
tagliatelle	1–2 minutes	2–3 minutes
tonnarelli	2–3 minutes	3–4 minutes
lasagne	2 minutes	4 minutes
stuffed shapes	5–6 minutes	7–9 minutes

As you can see from this chart, home-made pasta that has been left to dry takes longer to cook, as does shop-bought fresh pasta

DRIED PASTA

capelli d'angelo	5 minutes
spaghettini	6–7 minutes
spaghetti, bigoli, long maccheroni, bucatini, linguine	8–10 minutes
tagliatelle	8–10 minutes
conchigliette or small tubular shapes	8 minutes
gnocchi, ditali, orecchiette or any medium tubular shapes	8–10 minutes
penne, rigatoni or any large tubular shapes	9–12 minutes

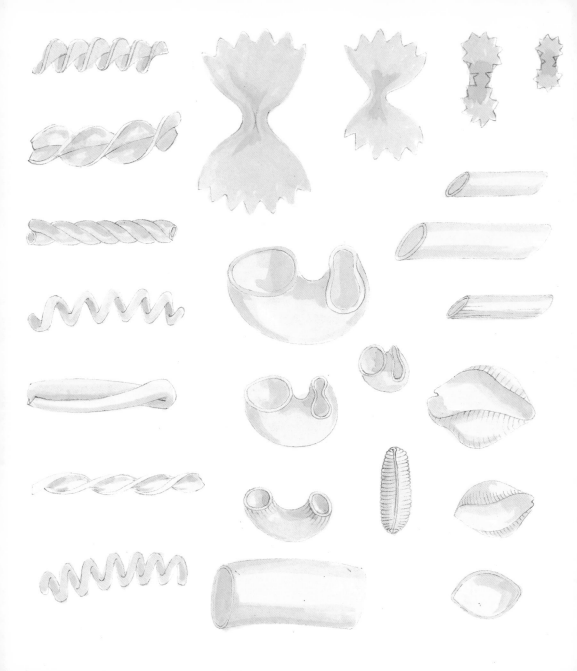

It is easy to cook pasta, but it can be spoiled by carelessness. Pasta needs to be cooked in a large saucepan and a lot of water – about 1 litre/1¾ pints for 100g/3½oz of pasta. Bring the water to the boil and then add cooking salt – about 1½ tablespoons for 4 litres/7 pints, which is the quantity needed for 300–500g/11oz–1lb 2oz of pasta. The water might seem too salty, but it is thrown away and is not absorbed by the pasta.

Slide all the pasta into the boiling water, stir with a wooden fork or spoon to separate the pasta shapes, and cover the pan so that the water returns to the boil as soon as possible. Remove the lid and adjust the heat so that the water boils briskly, but does not boil over. The pasta is ready when it is *al dente*, which means that it offers some resistance to the bite. The best test to see if the pasta is ready is to fish out a piece and pop it in your mouth. It is absolutely unnecessary to add cold water to pasta after cooking, as is sometimes suggested by non-Italian cookery writers.

THE AGNESI METHOD

When I went to Imperia many years ago to see over the Agnesi pasta factory, the late Vincenzo Agnesi told me the way he liked to cook pasta. Here is what I call the Agnesi method, which I find more suitable when I

have friends to dinner, since the pasta does not become overcooked if you leave it a minute too long in the pot. It also produces a dish of pasta that retains the characteristic flavour of semolina. The method is only suitable for factory-dried pasta.

Bring a large saucepan of water to the boil, add salt to taste and then add the pasta and stir. When the water has come back to the boil, cook for 1 minute, stirring frequently. Turn off the heat, put a turkish towel cloth over the pan and close with a tight-fitting lid. Leave for the same length of time that the pasta would take to cook by the normal method, i.e. if it were still boiling. When the time is up, drain the pasta.

DRAINING PASTA

Pasta should be drained as soon as it is *al dente* (literally, 'to the tooth'): you must be able to feel its texture when you bite into it. However, if the pasta is going to be cooked further, by baking or frying, drain it when it is still slightly undercooked. Pasta for salads should be even more *al dente*.

It is important to drain pasta properly. Use a colander that is large enough to contain all the pasta you have cooked, and that has three little feet to stand on in the sink. Tip the pasta in, give the colander two sharp shakes, and immediately turn the pasta into a heated bowl or dish, into the frying pan with the sauce or into the saucepan in which it was cooked. (You can toss it better in the hot pan, with no worry about making a mess.) Penne, gnocchi or any shapes that are hollow need more draining because water may be trapped in the hollows. However, pasta should never be overdrained, as it needs to be slippery for coating with the sauce. Do not leave it sitting 'naked' in the colander, like the Chinese and Japanese do with their noodles. It should be dressed as soon as it is drained.

In southern Italy they do not use a colander for long pasta. The spaghetti is lifted out of the pan with two long forks. It is kept in the air for only a few seconds for the excess water to run off and then immediately transferred to the frying pan or the serving bowl. The Neapolitans say *'Gli spaghetti devono avere la goccia'* – spaghetti must be still just dripping.

HOME-MADE PASTA

MAKING THE DOUGH

200g/7oz, approximately, plain white flour (preferably Italian 00)
semolina for dusting
2 size-2 free-range eggs
Makes about 350g/$\frac{3}{4}$lb pasta, enough for 4 people as a first course or 3 as a main course

Note: I recommend the use of Italian Grade 00 flour for making pasta dough. It is the best for this purpose because it absorbs the eggs more evenly, is easier to knead and roll out and, above all, makes pasta of a more fragrant flavour and a more delicate texture. Italian 00 flour is now available in most delicatessens and Italian specialist shops.

1 Put most of the flour on the work surface and make a well in the centre. Place the rest of the flour to one side. Break the eggs into the well. Beat them lightly with a fork for about 1 minute, then draw the flour in gradually from the inner wall of the well. I do this with two fingers because I find that gives me more control. When the eggs are no longer runny draw in enough flour to enable you to knead the dough. At this stage you might have to add the flour you set aside, and even a little more from the bag, which you should keep at hand. You should add enough flour so that the dough is no longer sticky. (It is not possible to give the exact amount of flour needed because it depends on the absorption capacity of the eggs and the humidity of the kitchen.) Work until the flour and eggs are thoroughly amalgamated, put the dough to one side and scrape the work surface clean. Wash and dry your hands.

Note: It is easier for a beginner to stretch a soft dough, though a dough that is too soft may stick and tear and become unmanageable. You can make a harder dough by replacing half the flour with fine semolina. This dough is difficult to roll out by hand, but it works all right in the hand-cranked machine. It makes a pasta that is less delicate and less smooth in texture, but with a definite flavour, particularly suitable for vegetable sauces.

2 Proceed to knead the dough by pressing and pushing with the heel of your palm, folding the dough back, giving it half a turn and repeating these movements. Repeat the movements for about 10 minutes if you are going to make your pasta by hand, or 2–3 minutes if you are going to use a machine. Wrap the dough in cling film and leave it to rest for at least 30 minutes, though you can leave it for up to 3 hours, or even overnight.

ROLLING OUT BY HAND

To roll out by hand you need, ideally, an Italian rolling pin, which is about 82cm/32in long and 3.7cm/1½in in diameter. If you do not have a *mattarello* – long, thin rolling pin – you must divide the dough and roll it out in two batches, so that the circle of rolled-out pasta does not become too large for your rolling pin.

ROLLING OUT BY MACHINE

I still think the hand-cranked machine is the best machine to use, and worth every penny of its very reasonable price. This is how to proceed.

Unwrap the dough and lightly dust the work surface with flour. Knead the dough, as before, for a further 2 minutes, then divide it into four equal parts. Take one piece of dough and carefully re-wrap the other pieces in cling film.

Set the rollers of the machine to the widest opening. Flatten the piece of dough slightly, so that it nearly reaches the width of the machine. Run it through the machine five or six times, folding the sheet over and giving it a 180° turn each time. When the dough is smooth, run the sheet, unfolded and without turning it, through all the settings, closing the rollers one notch at a time until you achieve the desired thickness. For good results it is very important that you push the sheet of dough through each setting. If the sheet tears or sticks to the machine, dust it on both sides with flour.

For tonnarelli (like spaghetti but square in section) stop the rolling out at the second from last setting. For tagliatelle or tagliolini stop at the last but one. For flat sheet pasta stop at the last setting. If the atmosphere is damp, dough rolled out too thin cannot be stuffed to make ravioli or other small shapes as, instead of drying, it becomes more and more soggy when filled with the stuffing. If you find this happening, stop rolling out at the last but one setting. Alternatively, I sometimes prefer to roll out the strip twice through the last but one setting. This makes the pasta just a little thinner, but not as thin as the last setting. Roll out the dough to the last setting only for lasagne or cannelloni.

LONG PASTA, ——— TAGLIATELLE, FETTUCCINE ——— TONNARELLI, TAGLIOLINI

Lay each sheet of pasta dough on a clean tea towel, letting about one-third of its length hang down over the edge of the work surface. Leave until the pasta is dry to the touch and slightly leathery, but still pliable. This process takes about 30 minutes, depending on the humidity of the atmosphere and the texture of the pasta, and is essential because it prevents the strands from sticking together. Feed each sheet through the broad cutters of the machine for tagliatelle or fettuccine, or through the narrow ones for tonnarelli or tagliolini.

Separate the cut strands or wind them

loosely round your hand to make nests. Spread them out on clean tea cloths, and lightly dust them with semolina. Do not use flour, as this would be absorbed into the dough. The pasta is now ready to be cooked, or it can be dried and then stored in an airtight tin or plastic bag. Be very careful how you handle it because dried home-made pasta is very brittle and breaks easily.

LASAGNE AND CANNELLONI

Proceed immediately to cut the shapes without drying the sheets. Cut each pasta sheet into squares of about 12×8.5cm/$5 \times 3\frac{1}{2}$in for lasagne, or 10×7.5cm/4×3in for cannelloni.

PAPPARDELLE

Roll out each sheet of pasta to the last but one notch of the hand-cranked machine. Leave the sheets to dry for no longer than 10 minutes and then cut into ribbons about $12–15$cm/$5–6$in long and 1.5cm/$\frac{3}{4}$in wide. Lay the pappardelle, not touching each other, on clean tea cloths.

STUFFED PASTA SHAPES

You must work straight away while the pasta dough is still fresh and pliable. Roll out the dough and stuff the sheets, one or two at a time, depending on the shape being made. Keep the remainder of the dough in cling film.

Cook the little shapes straight away or leave them until the next day, spread out on a clean cloth, dusted with semolina. Once dry, you can store stuffed pasta in plastic boxes, in layers interleaved with greaseproof paper. Do not keep them for longer than a day or the stuffing might be spoiled.

GREEN PASTA

The only coloured pasta I consider worth writing about is the traditional green pasta made with spinach. All the modern creations of red, black or brown pasta are gimmicks, and sometimes they spoil the flavour of the pasta. Flavour and colour should be added only by the sauce.

150g/5oz cooked fresh spinach, or frozen spinach, thawed and cooked for 5 minutes
225g/8oz plain white flour, preferably Italian 00
2 size-2 free-range eggs

Squeeze all the liquid out of the spinach with your hands. Chop it very finely with a knife. Do not use a food processor as the spinach would become like a liquid mass. Add the chopped spinach to the well in the flour together with the eggs, and knead and roll out as for normal pasta.

SAUCES FOR SHAPES

In Italy there are said to be 350 different shapes of pasta (I've never counted them!). Although you are unlikely to find such a vast number of pasta shapes outside Italy, there are now a very considerable number to choose from. The drawings on pages 6–7 are of the most common and easily available shapes. In the recipes I explain which shape of pasta is usually dressed with the sauce in question, but you do not have to follow my suggestions slavishly.

There are, however, certain basic rules that govern which pasta shapes should be dressed with which sauce. In general, long thin shapes are dressed with an olive oil-based sauce that allows the strands to remain slippery and separate. Typical recipes are spaghettini with oil, garlic and chilli (page 20) and the spaghetti with tomato sauce on page 19.

Thicker long shapes, such as ziti, tonnarelli, bucatini or fettuccine, are best in heavier sauces containing prosciutto or bits of meat, cheese and eggs. A prime example is the carbonara on page 37.

Medium-size short tubular pasta like ditali, orecchiette and fusilli are perfect with vegetable sauces of any kind, these being the shapes traditionally made in southern Italy where pasta is most often combined with vegetables.

Penne and maccheroni and other large tubular shapes, as well as home-made shapes such as garganelli and pappardelle, are the perfect foil for a rich meat *ragù* and for use in most baked dishes. A *ragù* bolognese is traditionally combined with tagliatelle, and the choice for a northern Italian pasta al gratin (page 48) is penne.

As for the proportion of sauce to pasta, an average of 2 generous tablespoons of well-reduced sauce per portion of pasta is a good general guide.

ARRANGEMENT OF RECIPES

The recipes in this book are grouped according to the main ingredient of the sauce. Thus tagliatelle with bolognese sauce will be found with other recipes whose sauces are based on fish and meat products, while penne with tomato sauce is with the other recipes for vegetable-based sauces, such as orecchiette with broccoli.

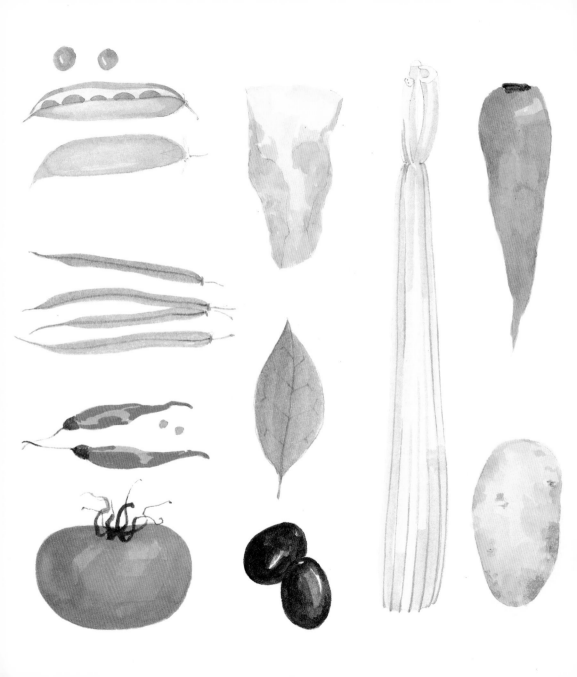

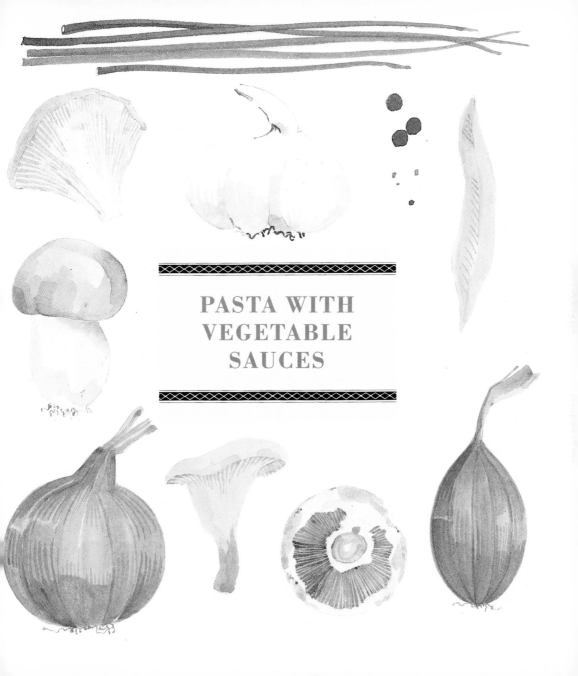

PASTA WITH VEGETABLE SAUCES

PESTO

PESTO SAUCE

30g/1oz pine nuts
90g/3oz fresh basil leaves
1 garlic clove, peeled
pinch of sea salt
4 level tbsp freshly
grated Parmesan
2 level tbsp freshly grated
aged pecorino
90ml/3fl oz extra virgin olive oil
40g/1½oz unsalted butter

Use young basil leaves for pesto; basil that has been growing for too long acquires an unpleasant strong taste. The pine nuts must be fresh, i.e. of the current year, and the oil must be a very good olive oil, although an unassertive one. If possible use an oil from Liguria or from Lake Garda (they can be found in Italian delicatessens); they are less pungent than a Tuscan oil, and less herby than an oil from Apulia.

The oil must be added slowly, as for mayonnaise, so as to create the right thickness. Some cooks add walnuts as well as pine nuts, but I prefer to add only pine nuts in order to keep the emphasis on the fresh flavour of the basil. If you have time, make your pesto by hand in a mortar; more juices are released than would be by the chopping action of the metal blade in a food processor or blender. I add a little softened butter to the pesto just before serving, to make the sauce sweeter and more delicate. Before tossing the pesto with the pasta, always dilute it with 3 or 4 tablespoons of the water in which the pasta has been cooking.

1 Heat the oven to 180°C/350°F/Gas Mark 4. Spread the pine nuts on a baking tray and toast in the oven for 5 minutes or so. This will bring out the flavour of the nuts.

2 To make in a mortar:
Put the basil leaves, garlic, pine nuts and salt in the mortar. Grind against the sides of the mortar with the pestle, crushing the ingredients until the mixture has become a paste. Mix in the grated cheeses. Add the oil gradually, beating with a wooden spoon.

To make in a food processor or blender:
Cut the garlic into thin slices and drop them into the container of

the food processor or blender. Add the basil, pine nuts, salt and oil and process to a creamy consistency. Transfer the sauce to a bowl and mix in the cheeses.

3 Melt the butter over the lowest heat and blend into the pesto.

Pesto freezes very well. Omit the garlic and the cheeses and add them just before you are going to use the sauce.

PICAGGE AL PESTO
———————— PICAGGE WITH PESTO SAUCE ————————

In Liguria, the motherland of pesto, potato and a handful of French beans are cooked with the pasta. The pasta I like to use with pesto is picagge, a Ligurian word meaning ribbons. Picagge are half the width of lasagne, but the same length.

———————

1 Cut the pasta dough into strips about 5 × 12cm/2 × 5in. You can cut this shape as soon as you have rolled it out; you do not have to let the pasta dry.

2 Cook the potatoes in their skins in boiling salted water. Drain, then peel and slice them. Put in a bowl.

3 Top and tail the beans. Cook them in plenty of boiling salted water until tender and then drain. Add to the potatoes. Toss with 3 or 4 tbsp of the pesto.

4 Cook the pasta in plenty of boiling salted water until *al dente*. Drain, reserving a cupful of the water, and return to the pan. Add 2 or 3 tbsp of the water to the pesto.

5 Toss the pasta with half the pesto. Transfer half the pasta to a serving dish. Spoon over the potato and bean mixture and cover with the rest of the pasta. Spread over the remaining pesto.

Home-made pasta keeps well in a hot oven for 15 minutes or so.

Serves 4 as a main course

home-made pasta dough, made with 3 size-2 eggs and 300g/11oz flour (page 9), or 500g/1lb 2oz bought linguine or fettuccine
3 small new potatoes
225g/½lb young French beans
pesto sauce from the preceeding recipe

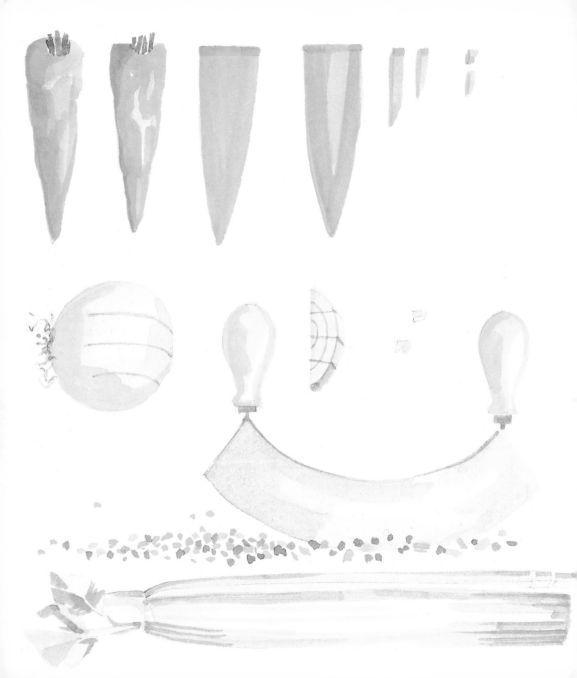

PASTA AL SUGO

PASTA WITH TOMATO SAUCE

The first tomato sauce here is denser and darker than the second one because of the many sautéed vegetables. I like it best for dressing a dish of penne or bucatini, although it is suitable for most dried pasta.

1 Sauté slowly the onion, carrot and celery in the olive oil until well softened (at least 10 minutes). Add the garlic and chilli just a few minutes before you finish the *soffritto* (sautéed mixture).
2 Add the chopped tomatoes, the herbs and sugar. Season lightly with salt and pepper.
3 Allow to simmer gently, uncovered, for 30–40 minutes, until the oil begins to separate out into small drops around the edge. Stir occasionally to prevent the sauce sticking to the bottom.
4 Remove and discard the parsley stalks and the bayleaf, and push the sauce through the coarsest disc of a mouli. Put the sauce in a saucepan. When the pasta is nearly ready, heat the sauce.
5 Cook the pasta in plenty of boiling salted water until *al dente*. Drain well and toss with the sauce. Serve at once, and hand round a bowl of freshly grated Parmesan.

A simpler and fresher tomato sauce can be made in the summer when good fresh tomatoes are on the market.

Peel, seed and coarsely chop 900g/2lb of ripe tomatoes and put them in a large heavy-bottomed sauté pan with 5 tbsp extra virgin olive oil, 6 garlic cloves, bruised, salt and freshly ground black pepper, a dozen snipped fresh basil leaves or $\frac{1}{2}$ tbsp of dried oregano. Cook briskly for 5 minutes, stirring frequently, until a lot of the tomato water has evaporated. Remove and discard the garlic before serving.

Serves 6 as a first course or 4 as a main course

1 medium-size onion, very finely chopped
1 medium-size carrot, very finely chopped
1 celery stick, very finely chopped
4 tbsp olive oil
1 garlic clove, very finely chopped
1 small dried chilli, seeded and chopped (optional)
800g/1¾lb Italian canned plum tomatoes, coarsely chopped
4 parsley stalks
1 bayleaf
1 tsp dried oregano
1 tsp sugar
salt and freshly ground black pepper
500g/1lb 2oz tubular pasta, such as penne or rigatoni
freshly grated Parmesan, to serve

SPAGHETTINI AGLIO OLIO E PEPERONCINO

—— THIN SPAGHETTI WITH OIL, GARLIC AND CHILLI ——

Serves 4 as a first course or
3 as a main course

350g/¾lb thin spaghetti
(spaghettini)
salt
120ml/4fl oz extra virgin
olive oil
3 garlic cloves, sliced
1 or 2 dried chillies,
according to taste,
seeded and crumbled

This sauce differs from that in Tagliatelle with Butter and Parmesan (page 52), in a way that demonstrates the essential difference between the cooking of northern Italy and that of the South. The aggressive flavour of this dish shows all the characteristics of Mediterranean cooking, while the delicate, but certainly not bland, Tagliatelle with Butter epitomises northern Italian cooking with its abundant use of butter and Parmesan.

1 Cook the pasta in plenty of boiling salted water, remembering that spaghettini will cook in about 6 minutes.
2 Meanwhile, put the oil, garlic and chillies in a frying pan large enough to hold all the pasta later. Cook for 1 minute over low heat. As soon as the garlic aroma rises, the sauce is ready. Draw off the heat immediately or the garlic might burn; this would ruin the taste of the oil.
3 Drain the pasta as soon as it is *al dente*. Do not overcook it. Transfer the pasta immediately to the frying pan. Stir-fry for a minute or so, using two forks and lifting the spaghetti high into the air so that every strand is beautifully glistening with oil. Serve at once, preferably straight from the pan.

No cheese is needed for this typically Neapolitan quick pasta.

PAPARELE E BISI

TAGLIATELLE WITH PEAS

'**P**aparele' and '*bisi*' are the Venetian dialect words for wide tagliatelle and *piselli*, peas, which are one of the Venetians' favourite vegetables. Here they are used to dress fresh tagliatelle in a delicate, well-balanced sauce. The sauce is also suitable for dressing a dish of dried farfalle.

1 Put half the butter, the pancetta and the onion in a small saucepan and sauté until the onion is soft and golden.

2 Mix in the peas and the parsley and then pour over the stock. Stir and add salt and pepper to taste. Cover the pan and cook over gentle heat until the peas are tender. The sauce should be quite thin.

3 Meanwhile, cook the pasta in plenty of boiling salted water until it is *al dente*. Drain and return to the pan.

4 Toss the pasta with the rest of the butter, pour over the sauce and mix in the Parmesan.

Serves 6 as a first course or 4 as a main course

60g/2oz butter
60g/2oz unsmoked pancetta, chopped
1 tbsp finely chopped onion
300g/10oz cooked peas, or frozen petits pois, thawed
1 tbsp chopped fresh flat-leaf parsley
120ml/4fl oz meat stock
salt and freshly ground black pepper
home-made tagliatelle, made with 3 size-2 eggs and 300g/11oz flour (page 9), or 500g/1lb 2oz bought fresh tagliatelle
60g/2oz Parmesan, freshly grated

ORECCHIETTE CON I BROCCOLI

PASTA WITH BROCCOLI

Serves 4 as a first course or
3 as a main course

450g/1lb broccoli
salt and freshly ground
black pepper
350g/¾lb orecchiette or other
medium-size pasta, or
wholemeal spaghetti
2 garlic cloves, peeled
1 dried chilli, seeded
3 salted anchovies, boned and
rinsed, or 6 canned anchovy
fillets, drained
6 tbsp extra virgin olive oil
4 tbsp freshly grated
aged pecorino

The combination of vegetables and pasta has its origins in Southern Italy. In Apulia this broccoli sauce is always served with orecchiette, which means 'little ears' because of their hollow shape. Orecchiette are made at home there, with semolina, flour and water. They are now produced commercially by the best Italian pasta manufacturers and are generally available within Italy and elsewhere.

I find that this sauce, as well as being good with orecchiette, is also one of the few that can stand up to the nutty flavour of brown pasta made with wholemeal flour (a flavour of which, like most Italians, I am not particularly fond). Wholemeal pasta is made in a number of shapes, among which spaghetti is by far the most successful.

1 Trim the broccoli. Divide into small florets and cut the stalks into 2.5cm/1in rounds.

2 Bring a large saucepan of water to the boil. Add about $1\frac{1}{2}$ tbsp of cooking salt and then slide in the broccoli. Stir well and cook for 5 minutes after the water has come back to the boil. Retrieve the broccoli from the water with a slotted spoon and lay them on kitchen paper towels. Pat dry and set aside.

3 Bring the broccoli water back to the boil and add the pasta. Cook in the usual way until very *al dente*.

4 While the pasta is cooking, chop the garlic, chilli and anchovy fillets together and sauté them in half the oil for 2 minutes, using a large frying pan. Mix in the broccoli and sauté for a few minutes, turning constantly.

5 When the pasta is done, drain and turn it into the frying pan. Stir-fry for a minute, then taste and check the seasoning.

6 Before you serve the pasta, pour over the rest of the olive oil and mix in the pecorino. If you like you can serve a bowl of freshly grated Parmesan on the side, although I find that the pecorino gives the dish enough of a cheesey taste.

TAGLIATELLE COL SUGO DI FUNGHI

TAGLIATELLE WITH MUSHROOM SAUCE

Serves 6 as a first course or
4 as a main course

30g/1 oz dried porcini
450g/1lb mixed fresh
mushrooms: cultivated
mushrooms, oyster
mushrooms, brown mushrooms
(champignons de Paris)
75g/2½oz butter
4 shallots, very finely chopped
salt and freshly ground
black pepper
1 garlic clove, finely chopped
1 tbsp chopped fresh parsley
1 tbsp chopped fresh marjoram,
or 2 tsp dried marjoram
2 tsp tomato purée
1 tbsp flour
225ml/8fl oz meat stock
150ml/¼pt dry white wine
about ¼ of a nutmeg, grated
home-made tagliatelle, made
with 3 size-2 eggs and
300g/11oz flour (page 9), or
700g 1½lb bought fresh
tagliatelle
freshly grated Parmesan, to
serve (optional)

I have adapted an old family recipe to suit the mushrooms that are available in this country. Admittedly there are more and more species of mushrooms in the shops, but they are not equally available in all parts of the country. The other reason why I have adapted the Italian recipe is that the sauce is so good that I want to be able to make it at any time of the year, and not only when the wild mushrooms are in season.

The woody, leafy perfume of *ceps* is given here by the dried porcini (ceps), which you can easily buy in Italian delicatessens and many supermarkets. To these you add a selection of cultivated mushrooms for a sweeter flavour and for texture.

---

1 Put the dried porcini in a bowl and cover with very hot water. Set aside to soak for 30 minutes or so and then lift them out. If they still have some grit, rinse under cold water. Dry and chop them. Filter the liquid through a muslin-lined sieve and reserve.
2 Clean the fresh mushrooms by wiping them with damp kitchen paper towels. If they are very dirty, rinse them under cold water. Dry and chop them coarsely. (I use a food processor which I pulsate for only a few seconds.)
3 Put half the butter and the shallots in a large sauté pan, add a pinch of salt and cook until the shallots are soft. Stir in the garlic and the herbs and sauté for a further minute. Add the tomato purée and cook for 30 seconds. Add the dried porcini, sauté for 5 minutes and then add the fresh mushrooms. Sauté over moderate heat for 5 minutes, turning the mushrooms over and over to *insaporire* – take up the flavour. Season with a little more salt and with a generous grinding of pepper. Turn the heat down and cook for a further 5 minutes.

4 Melt the remaining butter in a heavy saucepan and blend in the flour. Add the stock, stirring constantly and hard until well blended.

5 Heat the wine and add to the butter and stock mixture together with the nutmeg. Add some of the filtered porcini liquid, just enough to add mushroom flavour to the sauce, but not too much because it can be overpowering. Continue cooking very gently for about 15 minutes. Stir in the mushroom mixture. Check the seasoning and cook over the lowest possible heat for about 10 minutes.

6 Meanwhile, cook the tagliatelle in plenty of boiling salted water until *al dente*. Drain, but do not overdrain, reserving a cupful of the pasta water.

7 Turn half the pasta into a heated bowl and toss with half the mushroom sauce. Cover with the rest of the pasta and mix in the remaining sauce. If the pasta seems too dry, add 2–3 tbsp of the reserved water. Remember that fresh pasta absorbs a lot of liquid while it is sitting in the bowl. Serve at once with the optional cheese.

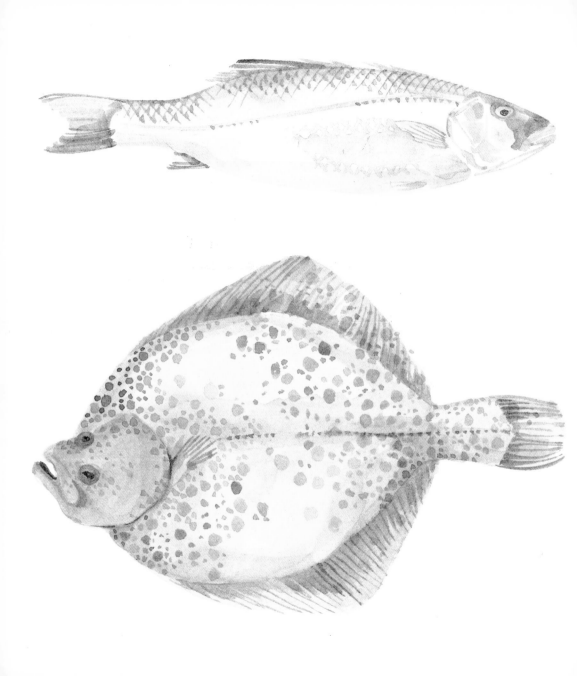

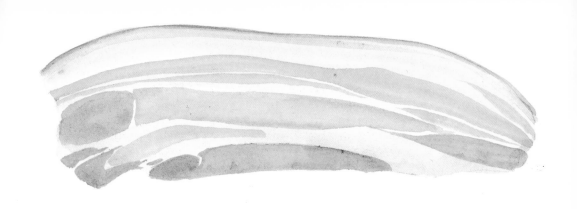

PASTA WITH MEAT & FISH SAUCES

TONNARELLI ALLA PURE DI TONNO
TONNARELLI WITH TUNA AND ANCHOVY PURÉE

Serves 4 as a first course or
3 as a main course

200g/7oz Italian or Spanish
canned tuna packed in olive oil,
drained
1½ salted anchovies,
boned and rinsed, or
3 canned anchovy fillets
3 tbsp pine nuts
3 tbsp freshly grated Parmesan
salt and freshly ground
black pepper
4 tbsp extra virgin olive oil
home-made tonnarelli, made
with 2 size-2 eggs and
200g/7oz flour (page 9), or
350g/¾lb bought fresh
tagliatelle

'There she goes again!' they say, when I hold forth about canned tuna. In most supermarkets the tuna on sale is skipjack tunny fish, an inferior fish, smaller in size and coarser in taste than the Mediterranean tunny. I strongly advise you to buy Italian or Spanish tuna packed in olive oil, which is available in most delicatessens. It is more expensive, but it is a very superior product. And it is absolutely necessary for this delicate creamy sauce.

Tonnarelli are a kind of square home-made pasta, particularly suitable for a smooth fish sauce.

1 Put the tuna, anchovies, pine nuts, cheese and pepper to taste in a food processor. Process while gradually adding the olive oil.
2 Slide the pasta into a saucepan of boiling water, to which only 1 tbsp salt has been added. (The sauce is quite salty.) Cook until *al dente*.
3 Scoop out a cupful of the pasta water and add about 6 tbsp of it to the sauce through the hole in the lid of the processor. The sauce should have the consistency of a thin béchamel. Taste and check the pepper.
4 Drain the tonnarelli and turn it into a heated bowl. Pour the sauce over it and toss thoroughly. Serve immediately.

BUCATINI ALL'AMATRICIANA
BUCATINI WITH SMOKED PANCETTA AND TOMATO SAUCE

Amatrice is a town on the central Apennines where on 15th August huge cauldrons of this dish are prepared for the local *festa*. The sauce is traditionally made with pork jowl, and flavoured with a lot of dried chilli and grated pecorino to counterbalance the fattiness of the meat. In this country I use smoked pancetta which I buy in a thick piece.

1 Put the pancetta and the oil in a non-stick frying pan and sauté until the fat has run out of the pancetta and the pancetta is crisp and browned. Stir frequently.

2 Add the onion and a pinch of salt to the frying pan and sauté for about 10 minutes. Mix in the garlic and chilli. Cook for a further minute or so and then splash in the wine. Turn the heat up and let the wine bubble away to reduce it by half. Pour in the tomato sauce and simmer for 15 minutes to allow the flavours to combine. Add salt and add pepper to your liking.

3 Cook the bucatini in plenty of boiling salted water until *al dente*. Drain thoroughly, giving the colander a few sharp shakes so that the water trapped in the bucatini comes out. Transfer the pasta to a heated bowl and mix in three-quarters of the sauce and the pecorino. Toss very thoroughly and then spoon over the rest of the sauce. Serve immediately, handing round the Parmesan separately in a bowl.

Serves 6 as a first course or 4 as a main course

350g/¾lb smoked pancetta, cut into 1cm/½in cubes
1 tbsp olive oil
1 small onion, very finely chopped
salt and freshly ground black pepper
1 garlic clove, finely chopped
1 dried chilli, seeded and finely chopped
120ml/4fl oz dry white wine
450ml/¾pt tomato sauce (page 19, bottom)
450g/1lb bucatini
6 tbsp freshly grated aged pecorino
freshly grated Parmesan to serve

TAGLIOLINI VERDI COL SALMONE E I FUNGHI

GREEN TAGLIOLINI WITH A SALMON AND
MUSHROOM SAUCE

Serves 3 or 4

20g/$\frac{3}{4}$oz dried porcini
350g/$\frac{3}{4}$lb piece of fresh salmon
250ml/9fl oz fish or
vegetable stock
120ml/4fl oz dry white wine
75g/2$\frac{1}{2}$oz unsalted butter
1 shallot, very finely chopped
salt and freshly ground
black pepper
180g/6oz cultivated fresh
mushrooms, cleaned and
coarsely chopped
1$\frac{1}{2}$ tbsp flour
3 tbsp double cream
home-made green tagliolini,
made with 2 size-2 eggs,
225g/8oz flour
and 150g/5oz cooked or frozen
spinach (page 9), or 450g/1lb
bought green tagliolini
bunch of fresh dill, chopped
freshly grated Parmesan,
to serve

In no way can I claim this to be a traditional Italian dish. It is an Anna Del Conte invention, good enough to pass on. It is definitely a *piatto unico* (one-course meal), with a good salad to be served afterwards, but not with it.

1 Put the dried porcini in a small bowl and cover with very hot water. Set aside to soak for about 30 minutes.
2 Meanwhile, put the salmon in a saucepan and cover with the stock and wine. Bring to the boil and boil for 1 minute. Remove from the heat and leave the salmon in the pan to finish cooking while you prepare the sauce.
3 Put half the butter and the shallot in a heavy saucepan. Sprinkle with a little salt and cook gently until the shallot is soft, stirring occasionally.

4 Lift the porcini out of the soaking water. If they are very dirty, rinse them under cold water. Dry and chop them coarsely. Filter the porcini liquid through a sieve lined with muslin to catch any grit, and reserve.

5 Add the chopped porcini to the shallot and sauté gently for 5 minutes. Mix in the cultivated mushrooms, turn the heat up and cook until the liquid has come out of the mushrooms. Stir frequently.

6 Lift the fish out of the stock and place it on a board. Strain the stock and reserve.

7 Blend the flour into the mushroom sauce and cook for a minute or so, stirring constantly. Pour over a cupful of the fish stock and stir rapidly over very low heat until smoothly blended. Add the rest of the stock very gradually, stirring constantly. Add 2–3 tbsp of the filtered porcini liquid. The sauce should be quite thin.

8 Bring the sauce slowly to the boil, then turn the heat right down, so that only a few bubbles break the surface of the sauce every now and then, and cook for 30 minutes. I use a flame diffuser. Alternatively you can cook the sauce in a bain-marie: place the pan containing the sauce in another saucepan of gently simmering water. You can of course simmer your mushroom sauce for only 5 minutes, but you will not achieve the same velvety, delicate yet rich sauce. At the end mix in the cream. Taste and adjust the seasoning.

9 Skin and bone the fish and flake the flesh. Add to the sauce and keep warm.

10 Cook the tagliolini in plenty of boiling salted water until *al dente*. Drain and return them to the hot saucepan in which they cooked. Toss with the remaining butter. Transfer to a heated bowl and cover with the sauce. Sprinkle the dill over the top just before serving. Pass the grated Parmesan round in a bowl.

TAGLIATELLE AL RAGU

TAGLIATELLE WITH BOLOGNESE SAUCE

Serves 6 as a first course or
4 as a main course

For the bolognese sauce
30g/1oz butter
3 tbsp extra virgin olive oil
60g/2oz unsmoked pancetta or
streaky bacon, finely chopped
1 small onion, finely chopped
$\frac{1}{2}$ carrot, finely chopped
1 celery stick, finely chopped
1 garlic clove, finely chopped
1 bayleaf
350g/$\frac{3}{4}$lb lean chuck or
braising beef, minced
1 tbsp tomato purée
150ml/$\frac{1}{4}$pt red wine
150ml/$\frac{1}{4}$pt meat stock
2 pinches of grated nutmeg
salt and freshly ground
black pepper
home-made tagliatelle, made
with 3 size-2 eggs and
300g/11oz flour (page 9) or
700g/1$\frac{1}{2}$lb bought fresh
tagliatelle
freshly grated Parmesan,
to serve

Bolognese sauce is out of fashion. A great pity, although I quite understand why.

The early emigrants from southern Italy to the USA took their beloved spaghetti with them. In America, when they opened their restaurants, they realised that the locals were great meat lovers. Thus, instead of introducing spaghetti with the traditional tomato sauce, the Italians had the clever idea – financially clever, but not gastronomically – of serving spaghetti with a meat sauce or meat balls. The meat sauce was a watered-down version, both literally and figuratively, of the *ragù bolognese*.

It quickly caught on, and spaghetti bolognese became synonymous with Italian cooking. But in fact there is no combination of pasta and sauce that is less typically Italian!

In Bologna, *ragù* is used to dress the local pasta – tagliatelle, not spaghetti – fresh, home-made with eggs and local soft-wheat flour. And what a wonderful dish it is. If you cannot afford the time to make your own tagliatelle, choose good fresh pasta. Remember that dried egg tagliatelle made by a reputable Italian producer are often better than fresh pasta made with inferior flour, a minimum of eggs and a lot of water.

1 To make the bolognese sauce, heat the butter and oil in a heavy saucepan and cook the pancetta for 2 minutes, stirring constantly. 2 Add the onion, and when it has begun to soften add the carrot, celery, garlic and bayleaf. Cook for a further 10 minutes, stirring frequently.

3 Put in the minced beef and cook to brown it as much as possible, crumbling it in the pan with a fork. Do this over high heat so that the meat browns rather than stews.

4 Add the tomato purée and continue to cook over high heat for a further 2 minutes. Still over high heat, splash in the wine and boil to evaporate. Remove and discard the bayleaf and pour in the stock. Season with the nutmeg, salt and pepper. Mix well and simmer, uncovered, for about 2 hours. Stir occasionally and add a little hot water if the sauce is too dry. The ragù should cook very slowly indeed, at the lowest possible simmer.

5 Cook the pasta in plenty of boiling salted water. Fresh pasta cooks quickly, so stay around and test after $1\frac{1}{2}$ minutes. Drain as soon as it is *al dente*, reserving a cupful of the pasta water.

6 Return half the pasta to the hot saucepan and stir in about half the *ragù*. Pour in the rest of the tagliatelle and the rest of the *ragù*. Mix very well, adding 2–3 tbsp of the reserved water if the pasta seems dry. Transfer to a heated bowl or deep dish and serve immediately, handing the cheese round separately.

PASTA CON LE SARDE

PASTA WITH FRESH SARDINES

Serves 4 as a main course

60g/2oz currants
6 tbsp extra virgin olive oil
1 red or Spanish onion, very
finely sliced
salt and freshly ground
black pepper
4 tbsp pine nuts
200g/7oz wild or cultivated
fennel leaves
2 salted anchovies,
boned and rinsed, or
4 canned anchovy fillets
450g/1lb fresh sardines, boned
(see Note opposite)
1 tsp fennel seeds
350g/¾lb bucatini

This dish from Sicily is like a history of that island in microcosm: part Greek, part Saracen, part Norman. The sardines and the wild fennel, typical food of the ancient Greeks, are here used to dress the most Italian of all foods, pasta. The dressing is lightened and made more interesting by the inclusion of pine nuts and currants, a Saracen influence, and the finished dish is cooked in the oven, a method brought to the island by the Normans. If you cannot get hold of wild or cultivated fennel leaves, use a small fennel bulb, cut into strips, together with its feathery green top.

1 Soak the currants in warm water for 10 minutes. Drain and dry well with kitchen paper towels.

2 Put 2 tbsp of the oil in a frying pan, add the onion and a pinch of salt, and sauté gently for 15 minutes, stirring frequently, until soft. Mix in the currants and the pine nuts and cook for a further 2 minutes.

3 Meanwhile, blanch the fennel leaves in a large saucepan of boiling salted water for 1 minute. (If you are using fennel bulb, cook until soft.) Lift the fennel out of the water with a slotted spoon, drain and dry with kitchen paper towels. Reserve the water in which it has cooked. Chop the fennel and add to the onion mixture. Cook over very low heat for 10–15 minutes, adding 2–3 tbsp of the fennel water whenever the mixture appears too dry.

4 Heat the oven to 200°C/400°F/Gas Mark 6.

5 Chop about half the sardines and the anchovies and add to the pan with the fennel seeds and a generous grinding of pepper. Cook gently for 10 minutes, stirring frequently and adding more fennel water whenever necessary. Taste and adjust the seasoning.

6 Heat 2 tbsp of the remaining oil in a non-stick frying pan. When the oil is very hot, but not yet smoking, slide in the remaining whole sardines and fry on both sides for 5 minutes.

7 Meanwhile, cook the pasta in the fennel water until very *al dente*. Drain, return the pasta to the pan and dress immediately with the sardine sauce.

8 Grease an oven dish with a little oil and transfer the pasta to it. Lay the fried sardines over the pasta, dribble with the rest of the oil and cover with foil. Bake for 15 minutes.

The dish can be prepared a few hours in advance and then baked for an extra 15 minutes to heat the pasta through.

Note: To clean and bone fresh sardines, snap off the head of each fish and pull it away, thus removing most of the inside. Remove the back fin by pulling it off, starting from the tail end. Hold the sardine with one hand and open the belly with the thumb of the other hand, running it against the spine on both sides. Open the fish, butterfly-fashion, and pull the spine sharply from the head end towards the tail end, giving a last sharp tug to remove the tail. Wash and dry the boned fish.

PAPPARDELLE CON LA LEPRE

PAPPARDELLE WITH HARE

Serves 5 or 6 as a main course

2 tbsp olive oil
75g/2½oz unsalted butter
30g/1oz unsmoked pancetta, chopped
1 small onion, very finely chopped
1small celery stick, very finely chopped
1 garlic clove, finely chopped
a small sprig of fresh rosemary, finely chopped
the legs of 1 hare
150ml/¼pt red wine
2 level tsp flour
150ml/¼pt meat stock
salt and freshly ground black pepper
pinch of grated nutmeg
2 tbsp double cream
home-made pappardelle, made with 3 size-2 eggs and 300g/11oz flour (page 9), or 400g/14oz dried tagliatelle, or 500g/1lb 2oz bought fresh tagliatelle

Only the legs of the hare are used for this dish. You can roast the saddle as they do in Tuscany, which is where this dish originally comes from. It is a rich dish, and is regarded as a *piatto unico* – one-course meal – even in Italy, where pasta is usually only the first course.

1 Heat the oil and half the butter in a sauté pan and cook the pancetta for 2 minutes, stirring constantly. Add the onion and sauté for a further 5 minutes, stirring very frequently. Add the celery, garlic and rosemary and cook until soft. Push the *soffritto* to one side of the pan.

2 Add the hare legs and brown well on all sides. Raise the heat, pour over the wine and boil until the liquid has reduced by half.

3 Transfer the hare to a plate. Stir the flour into the cooking juices. Cook for 1 minute and then pour in half the stock. Mix well. Return the hare to the pan and season with salt and nutmeg. Turn the heat down to very low and cook gently for a good hour, and the lid slightly askew. If the sauce gets too dry add a little of the remaining stock. The sauce should in the end be rather thick.

4 Remove the hare from the pan. Bone the legs and cut the meat into very small pieces. Return the meat to the pan and add the cream and pepper to taste. Cook for about 2 minutes, stirring constantly. Taste and adjust the seasoning, then remove from the heat. Reheat the sauce before adding to the pasta.

5 Cook the pasta in plenty of boiling salted water until *al dente*, remembering that if you are using fresh home-made pasta it will only take about 1 minute to cook. Drain and turn the pasta into a heated bowl. Add the remaining butter and spoon over the hot hare sauce. Serve at once.

SPAGHETTI ALLA CARBONARA

SPAGHETTI WITH EGGS AND BACON

The creation of this dish is attributed to the *carbonari* – charcoal burners – who used to make their charcoal in the mountainous forests of Lazio. Traditionally, the meat used was the jowl of the pig, but nowadays most carbonara is made with pancetta, which is belly of pork, similar to streaky bacon but differently cured.

1 Heat the oil, sage leaves and garlic clove in a large frying pan. Add the pancetta and sauté for about 10 minutes, until the pancetta is golden brown and the fat has run out. Discard the garlic and the sage.

2 Cook the spaghetti in plenty of boiling salted water until *al dente*.

3 Meanwhile, lightly beat the eggs in a bowl and add the Parmesan, a little salt and a generous amount of black pepper.

4 Drain the pasta, reserving a cupful of the water. Return the spaghetti to the saucepan and toss with the butter, then add to the frying pan. Stir-fry for a minute or so.

5 Remove from the heat and transfer the spaghetti mixture to a heated bowl. Pour over the egg and cheese mixture and add about 4 tbsp of the reserved water to give the sauce the right fluidity. Mix well and serve at once.

Serves 3 as a main course or
4 as a first course

1 tbsp olive oil
4 fresh sage leaves
1 garlic clove, peeled
120g/4oz smoked pancetta or
smoked streaky bacon, cut into
matchsticks
350g/¾lb spaghetti
3 eggs
6 tbsp freshly grated Parmesan
salt and freshly ground
black pepper
60g/2oz butter

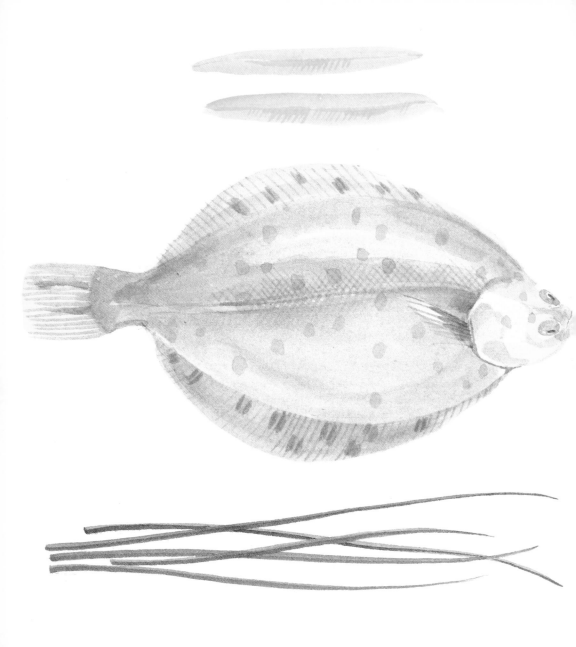

BAKED AND
STUFFED
PASTA

RAVIOLI DI PESCE

Serves 4 as a main course

For the pasta dough
200g/7oz white flour
(preferably Italian 00)
2 size-2 eggs
1 tsp olive oil
1 tbsp oil
90g/3oz unsalted butter
3 tbsp very finely cut fresh chives
freshly grated Parmesan, to serve

For the filling
60g/2oz unsalted butter
2 tbsp very finely chopped onion
300g/10 oz skinless white fish fillet, such as Dover sole, turbot, sea bass or sea bream
1 salted anchovy, boned and rinsed, or 2 canned anchovy fillets, drained
120ml/4fl oz dry white wine
150g/5oz fresh ricotta
4 tbsp double cream
3 tbsp freshly grated Parmesan
2 egg yolks
salt and freshly ground black pepper

A new type of ravioli and a successful one. You can use any firm-fleshed fish including, of course, cod. The better the fish, the more tasty the ravioli!

1 First prepare the filling: put the butter and onion in a saucepan and cook for 5 minutes, stirring and pressing the onion against the side of the pan to release the flavour.

2 Meanwhile, cut the fish into very small pieces. Chop the anchovy. Add both to the onion and cook for $1\frac{1}{2}$–2 minutes.

3 Turn the heat up and splash in the wine, then boil rapidly until it has totally evaporated. Flake the fish coarsely, transfer the mixture to a bowl and allow to cool for a few minutes.

4 Add the ricotta to the fish mixture with the cream, Parmesan and egg yolks. Season with salt and pepper and mix very well. Set aside while you make the pasta dough, following the instructions on page 9, adding the olive oil with the eggs.

5 Cut off one-quarter of the pasta dough, leaving the rest wrapped in cling film. Thin the dough down in the pasta machine notch by notch as far as the last but one notch, as described on page 11. If you are rolling out by hand, roll the dough out as thin as you possibly can.

6 Work on one strip of dough at a time, keeping the remaining strips covered with a tea cloth. Place mounds of the filling about $\frac{1}{2}$ tsp each in a straight line along the length of the strip of dough spacing them about 4cm/$1\frac{1}{2}$in apart and the same distance from the one long edge. Fold the dough lengthways over the filling and, using a pastry wheel, trim the edges where they meet. Then cut into squares between each mound of filling. Separate the squares and squeeze out any air that may be caught in the ravioli. Seal them tight with moistened fingers.

7 Place the ravioli on clean dry tea cloths, well separated. Cut off another quarter of the dough, knead in any trimmings from the previous batch and thin the strip down as before. If you are rolling out by hand keep the dough you are not working on well covered or it will dry up and become brittle. Continue making more ravioli until you have used up all the filling and/or all the dough. Leave the ravioli uncovered until they are properly dry; you can then cover them with another cloth.

8 Bring a large saucepan of water to the boil. Add the oil and $1\frac{1}{2}$ tbsp salt. Drop the ravioli gently into the pan and bring the water back to the boil. Adjust the heat so that the water boils gently; if it boils too fast the ravioli might break. Cook until they are done, about 4–5 minutes, stirring gently every now and then. The best way to tell if they are done is to try one: the pasta should be still firm to the bite, *al dente*, at the edge. Lift the ravioli out with a slotted spoon and transfer them immediately to a heated and buttered bowl. Pat them dry with kitchen paper towels.

9 While the ravioli are cooking, melt the butter in a small saucepan. Stir in the chives. Pour this sauce over the ravioli. Serve at once, handing round the grated Parmesan in a separate bowl.

LASAGNE AL FORNO

BAKED LASAGNE

Serves 4–6

home-made lasagne, made with
3 size-2 eggs and 300g/11oz
flour (page 9) or 700g/1½lb
bought fresh lasagne
Bolognese sauce
(page 32)
1 tbsp salt
1 tbsp vegetable or olive oil
75g/2½oz Parmesan,
freshly grated
15g/½oz butter

For the béchamel sauce
750ml/1¼pt full-fat milk
75g/2½oz unsalted butter
60g/2oz flour flavoured with
2 pinches of grated nutmeg

Few dishes have been so badly copied abroad as baked lasagne, a dish that surely has acquired an appalling image. Yet when well made it is one of the finest creations of the very rich Bolognese cuisine. While I might occasionally be pushed to use shop-bought fresh tagliatelle, I find shop-bought lasagne frankly not good enough.

This is a party dish, perfect for a family celebration. A certain amount of time must be set aside to prepare it. So try to do it properly and make your own pasta. The difference is quite remarkable.

1 If you are making your own lasagne, lay the pasta rectangles out, separate from each other, on clean tea towels.

2 While the bolognese sauce is cooking, make the béchamel. You will find the recipe on page 48.

3 Choose a large sauté pan. Fill it with water and add the salt and oil. When the water is boiling, slide in 5 or 6 lasagne at a time. Move them around with a wooden fork to stop them sticking to each other. When they are *al dente*, lift them out with a fish slice and plunge them into a bowl of cold water. Lift out, lay on cloths and pat dry with kitchen paper towels.

4 Heat the oven to 220°C/425°F/Gas Mark 7.

5 Butter a 30 × 20cm/12 × 8in ovenproof dish. Spread 2 tbsp of the bolognese sauce on the bottom. Cover with a layer of lasagne and spread over 2 tbsp or so of bolognese and the same of béchamel sauce. Sprinkle with a little Parmesan. Repeat, building up the dish in thin layers until you have used up all the ingredients. The top layer must be béchamel.

6 Dot with the butter and bake for 20 minutes. Remove from the oven and allow to rest for at least 5 minutes before serving so the flavours can develop.

IL RAVIOLONE

PASTA AND SPINACH ROLL

Serves 6 as a main course,
8 as a first course

700g/1½lb frozen leaf spinach,
thawed, or scant 1.35kg/3lb
fresh spinach
salt and freshly ground
black pepper
3 tbsp very finely chopped
shallots
30g/1oz unsalted butter
225g/8oz fresh ricotta
90g/3oz Parmesan, freshly
grated
½ tsp grated nutmeg
1 egg yolk
home-made pasta dough, made
with 200g/7oz flour, the yolks
of 4 size-2 eggs and just enough
cold water to help the dough
absorb the flour (page 9)
4 large slices of unsmoked ham

For dressing the roll
90g/3oz unsalted butter, heated
with 1 bruised garlic clove and
4–6 fresh sage leaves,
or a thin béchamel sauce
(see Note opposite)
freshly grated Parmesan

In this dish the procedure for stuffing pasta is different. The whole sheet of pasta dough is rolled around the spinach filling. The roll is sliced when cold, just like a meat joint, and then heated up in the oven with its sauce. It results in a very attractive presentation.

---

1 If you are using frozen spinach, cook the thawed spinach in a covered pan with a little salt for 5 minutes. If you are using fresh spinach, discard any wilted or discoloured spinach leaves and the tougher stalks. Wash it, and then cook in a covered pan with just the water that clings to the leaves and with a little salt for 5–8 minutes, or until tender. Drain the spinach, squeezing lightly to remove most of its moisture. Set aside.

2 In a frying pan, sauté the chopped shallot in the butter over moderate heat. When the shallot turns pale gold in colour, add the spinach and sauté for 5 minutes, turning the spinach over and over to *insaporire* – take up the flavour.

3 Transfer the contents of the frying pan to a food processor and add the ricotta, grated Parmesan, nutmeg, and, last of all, the egg yolk. Process for a few seconds. Check the seasoning.

4 Roll out the pasta dough into as thin a sheet as possible, about 50 × 37cm/20 × 15in. Lay it flat in front of you. Square the sides to make a neat rectangle.

5 Place the ham slices to cover the pasta rectangle completely, leaving a clean edge of about 2.5m/1in on all sides.

6 Spread the spinach filling over the ham. Roll up as for a Swiss roll by first making a pleat and then rolling fairly tightly. Wrap the pasta roll tightly in muslin and tie the two ends securely with string.

7 Use a fish kettle or other long, deep pan that can hold the roll comfortably and about 4 litres/7 pints of water. Bring the water to the boil, add about 2 tbsp of salt and then put in the pasta roll. Cook at a gentle but steady boil for 35 minutes.

8 Lift out the roll. Unwrap it while it is hot and set it aside to cool, loosely covered with foil.

9 Heat the oven to 200°C/400°F/Gas Mark 6.

10 Cut the roll into 1cm/$\frac{1}{2}$in slices with a very sharp knife or an electric knife. (It is easier to slice the *rotolo* when cool.)

11 Place the slices in a generously buttered shallow baking dish, overlapping them a little. You can dress the slices with either the garlic- and sage-flavoured butter and then a generous amount of Parmesan, or with a layer of Parmesan covered with the thin, well-flavoured béchamel. Cover the dish with foil and bake for 15–20 minutes. Remove from the oven and leave for 5 minutes before serving.

Note: For a thin béchamel, use 750ml/1$\frac{1}{4}$pt full-fat milk, 75g/2$\frac{1}{2}$oz unsalted butter and 45g/1$\frac{1}{2}$oz flour. Follow the recipe on page 48, heating the milk with 1 bayleaf.

PASTA 'NCACIATA

AUBERGINE AND RIGATONI CAKE

Serves 6 as a first course or
4–5 as a main course

2 aubergines, total weight about
450g/1lb
salt and freshly ground
black pepper
vegetable oil for frying
450g/1lb penne or rigatoni
60g/2oz butter
double quantity plain tomato
sauce (page 19 bottom)
225g/½lb Italian mozzarella
cheese, coarsely grated or
chopped
4 tbsp freshly grated Parmesan
4 tbsp freshly grated aged
pecorino
1 level tbsp dried oregano
2 tbsp dried white breadcrumbs

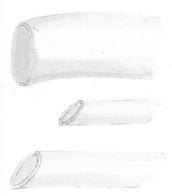

This is a very showy southern Italian dish traditionally baked in a dome-shaped container, which can be tricky to unmould. In this recipe I suggest using a springform tin. It can be prepared a few hours in advance.

1 Cut the aubergines into 6mm/¼in slices. Place a board on the slant over the sink. Put layers of aubergine slices on the board, sprinkling each layer with salt. Leave to drain for 1 hour. Rinse thoroughly and pat each slice dry.

2 Heat enough oil in a large frying pan to come about 2.5cm/1in up the sides of the pan. The oil is hot enough when a corner of an aubergine slice dipped into it sizzles. Slide in a few slices of aubergine at a time and fry until deep golden on both sides. Do not overcrowd the slices or they will not fry properly.

3 Remove the fried aubergines with a slotted spoon, drain well and place in a dish lined with kitchen paper towels.

4 Cook the rigatoni in plenty of boiling salted water until very *al dente*. Drain and return the rigatoni to the saucepan in which they were cooked and toss with the butter. Mix in the tomato sauce, the three cheeses, oregano and pepper to taste. Check the seasoning.

5 Heat the oven to 190°C/375°F/Gas Mark 5.

6 Line the bottom of a 20cm/8in springform cake tin with aubergine slices. Fill in any gaps with cut-up pieces of aubergine. Line the sides of the tin with aubergine slices, cutting to fit. Place any aubergine left over on the bottom of the tin. Fill the tin with the rigatoni mixture and press down lightly. Sprinkle with the breadcrumbs.

7 Bake for 20 minutes or until the filling is hot.

8 Remove from the oven and run a palette knife around the side of the tin. Place a heated round serving dish over the top of the tin and turn the tin upside down. Tap the base of the tin and give the dish a sharp shake or two. Unclip the ring and lift the tin away carefully. If necessary, press into place any pieces of aubergine stuck to the tin. Allow the cake to stand for at least 5 minutes for the flavours to combine.

PASTA AL GRATIN

MACARONI CHEESE

Serves 4 as a first course or
3 as a main course

60g/2oz fontina, grated
60g/2oz Parmesan,
freshly grated
350g/¾lb penne or maccheroni

For the béchamel sauce
750ml/1¼pt full-fat milk
75g/2½oz unsalted butter
60g/2oz flour
salt and freshly ground
black pepper
grated nutmeg

Years ago, at the beginning of my married life in England, my husband asked me which was my favourite pasta dish. 'Very difficult question,' I answered. Recently, however, when he asked me the same question, I said, 'Pasta al gratin.' 'Oh really?' he said, and thought, 'What about that discerning palate she's so proud of?' But he was thinking of the macaroni cheese of his school days, and I was thinking of the velvety, cheesey delight of Pasta al Gratin.

Although it is made with a sauce with a French name, the dish is Italian. It is made in many regions, with certain variations. In the North, for instance, Parmesan is used, sometimes mixed with emmental or with fontina, as in my recipe, while in Naples a buffalo mozzarella is cut up and pushed here and there among the penne.

For all its simplicity, Pasta al Gratin needs a careful and patient cook, able to make a velvety béchamel and to drain the pasta at the right time, i.e. when still slightly undercooked, so that it can reach the right texture during baking.

1 To make the béchamel sauce, heat the milk until hot but not boiling. Draw off the heat.
2 Melt the butter, draw the saucepan off the heat and stir in the flour. Put the pan back on the heat and cook, stirring constantly, for about half a minute.
3 Draw the pan off the heat and add the milk gradually. At the beginning add only a couple of tablespoons and incorporate well, before adding another few tablespoons. Adding the milk slowly in this way helps prevent the flour forming lumps. Return the pan to the heat and cook until the sauce comes to the boil. Season

with salt and pepper and with a generous grating of nutmeg. Cook for a few minutes, stirring constantly.

4 To finish the sauce you can either use a flame diffuser under the pan, or you can put the pan into a larger saucepan of simmering water – the bain-marie method. Leave the sauce to cook very, very gently for 30 minutes; you only need to stir occasionally. This long slow cooking makes a rich velvety sauce that you would not be able to achieve if you only cooked the béchamel for 5 minutes, that is, just enough to cook the flour.

5 Add the cheeses to the béchamel. Taste and adjust the seasoning.

6 Cook the pasta in plenty of boiling salted water until very *al dente*. Drain thoroughly (penne tend to hold water in their hollows).

7 Heat the oven to 180°C/350°F/Gas Mark 4.

8 Coat a shallow baking dish (about 5cm/2in deep) with a little of the sauce. Dress the pasta with about two-thirds of the béchamel and transfer to the prepared dish. Spread the rest of the sauce all over the top. Bake for about 30 minutes, until the penne at the top begin to brown.

9 Leave out of the oven for 5 minutes before serving, to allow the flavours to blend while cooling a little.

OTHER
FAVOURITES

TAGLIATELLE AL BURRO E FORMAGGIO
——— TAGLIATELLE WITH BUTTER AND PARMESAN ———

Serves 4 as a first course or
3 as a main course

home-made tagliatelle, made
with 2 size-2 eggs and
200g/7oz flour (page 9)
salt
60g/2oz Parmesan,
freshly grated
60g/2oz best quality unsalted
butter

In my home in Milan when I was a child, special butter was used for this sauce. The best farm butter was sold, cut in pieces and wrapped in muslin, by the best delicatessen in Via Monte Napoleone. And the tagliatelle were, of course, home-made.

This recipe is characteristic of northern Italian cooking. It is also the dressing used when you are lucky enough to have a white truffle to shave over it. To do the dish justice, you should make your own pasta and buy the best unsalted butter, as well as making sure your Parmesan is a proper Parmigiano Reggiano, of which you grate an ample quantity just before serving.

1 Cook the pasta in plenty of boiling salted water until *al dente*. Drain – but do not overdrain – and turn half the pasta into a heated serving bowl. Add about 4 tbsp of the cheese and stir well. **2** Cut the butter into small pieces and add half to the bowl. Toss thoroughly, then add the remaining cheese. Add the remaining butter and toss until all the butter has melted. Serve at once.

In Milan, more cheese is handed round separately in a bowl.

TAGLIOLINI PICCANTI FREDDI

TAGLIOLINI WITH A PIQUANT SUN-DRIED
TOMATO SAUCE

I do not usually like cold pasta, but I make a few exceptions. This is the best cold pasta dish I know, and it has always been a great success at my demonstrations.

When I have not got time to make my tagliolini, I prefer to use a good brand of dried tagliolini such as Cipriani or Spinosi, rather than shop-bought fresh pasta.

For this recipe buy loose sun-dried tomatoes that you reconstitute, not the kind under oil.

1 To reconstitute the sun-dried tomatoes, put them in a bowl. Heat 200ml/7fl oz of water with the wine vinegar, and when just boiling pour over the tomatoes. Leave to soak for at least 2 hours.
2 Lift the tomatoes out of the liquid, lay them on a wooden board and dry each one thoroughly with kitchen paper towels. Cut them into thin strips and put in a bowl large enough to hold the pasta later. Add the oil, chillies, garlic and basil.
3 Cook the tagliolini in plenty of boiling salted water. Drain it when it is even more *al dente* than you would like for eating it hot. (Overcooked cold pasta is really unpleasant.) Turn the pasta into the bowl and toss very thoroughly, lifting the strands up high so as to separate them. Leave to infuse for 2 hours or so, then fish out the garlic and discard. Scatter with the olives and serve.

Serves 4 as a first course

180g/6oz sun-dried tomatoes
120ml/4fl oz wine vinegar
6 tbsp extra virgin olive oil
1 or 2 dried chillies, according to taste, strength and size, seeded and crumbled
5 garlic cloves, bruised
a dozen fresh basil leaves, torn into small pieces
300g/11oz dried tagliolini, or home-made tagliolini made with 2 size-2 eggs and 200g/7oz flour (page 9)
salt
75g/2½oz black olives, such as Kalamata

TAGLIARDI E ZUCCHINE AL SUGO DI PISTACCHIO E BASILICO

TAGLIARDI AND COURGETTES WITH A PISTACHIO NUT AND BASIL SAUCE

Serves 6 as a first course or
4 as a main course

home-made green pasta dough,
made with 3 size-2 eggs,
350g/¾lb flour
and 225g/½lb cooked spinach
(page 9), or 250g/9oz bought
green tagliatelle or tagliardi
200ml/7 fl oz extra virgin olive
oil, preferably from
Sicily or Puglia
4 garlic cloves, bruised
600g/1¼lb courgettes, cut into
matchsticks
salt and freshly ground
black pepper
120g/4oz shelled pistachio nuts
50g/1¾oz fresh basil
30g/1oz fresh flat-leaf parsley
15g/½oz unsalted butter

Last year, during a short visit to Sicily, I had more interesting pasta dishes than during many a year in London. The pistachio and basil sauce was prepared for a dinner in the garden by Vittoria Spadaro, a friend and a good cook who is passionate about the great tradition of her island's cooking. The combination of flavours and the presentation of this dish epitomise the very best of Sicilian cooking.

The pasta used by Vittoria was green pappardelle which she made herself. If you do not have the time or inclination to make your own pasta I suggest you buy a box of the excellent tagliardi made by Cipriani, available in the best delicatessens. It is the best egg pasta on the market. It has a delicate silky texture which is normally found only in home-made pasta. Cipriani pasta is expensive, but when cooked it grows in volume more than any other pasta. And it is so good that it is well worth its higher price.

1 If you are making your own pasta, roll it and cut into pappardelle (page 12). Spread the pasta out on clean tea towels while you make the sauce.
2 Heat 2 tbsp of the oil and the garlic in a non-stick frying pan. When hot, add the courgettes and fry at a lively heat until golden all over. Shake the pan very often. They are ready whey they are tender, not still crunchy but not yet soft, and when the flavour has fully developed – about 15 minutes. Season with salt and pepper.
3 While the zucchini are frying, put the pistachios into a small saucepan. Cover with water, bring to a boil, and boil 10 seconds. Skin the pistachios, taking them out of the hot water a few at a

time for easier peeling. Dry them thoroughly and put in a food processor.

4 Rinse and dry the basil and parsley and add to the pistachios. Process while adding the rest of the oil through the hole in the lid. Stop the machine, push the mixture down from the side of the bowl, and process again a few seconds. Add salt and pepper to taste. Scoop out the mixture into a serving bowl and place the bowl in a warm oven.

5 Cook the pasta in plenty of salted boiling water until *al dente*. Drain, reserving a cupful of the pasta water, and turn immediately into the heated bowl. Add the butter and toss very thoroughly, adding 3 or 4 tablespoons of the reserved water to give the pasta the right fluidity.

6 Spoon the zucchini and their juices over the top of the pasta and serve at once.

CONCHIGLIE DI RADICCHIO ROSSO
COL RIPIENO DI PASTA
———— RED RADICCHIO LEAVES FILLED WITH PASTA ————

1 garlic clove
2 salted anchovies, boned and
rinsed or 4 canned anchovy
fillets, drained
1 dried chilli
4 tbsp extra virgin olive oil
salt
225g/½lb ditali or gnocchi
4 outside leaves from a large
head of red radicchio
freshly ground black pepper
(optional)

Although I am not very keen on pasta salads, I am not as hostile towards them as one woman evidently was, judging by a recent report in *The Times*.

'Laurette Bruson threw macaroni salad at Richard, her groom, during a tiff at their wedding reception in Tampa, Florida, and he responded by shooting her with a .22 pistol.'

This salad is an attractive dish, definitely not for throwing, with the shiny ditali tasting mainly of olive oil. I use a peppery oil for this dish, such as an extra virgin oil from Chianti or a fruity and herby oil from Sicily or Puglia.

If you cannot find a large radicchio head, use a Webb's or a round lettuce.

———

1 Chop the parsley, garlic and anchovies and put them in a large bowl together with the whole chilli. Beat in the oil and add salt to taste.

2 Cook the pasta in plenty of boiling salted water, remembering that cold pasta needs to be more *al dente* than hot pasta. Drain, refresh under cold water and drain again thoroughly. Pat dry with kitchen paper towels. Turn the pasta into the bowl with the dressing and toss well. Leave to infuse for about 2 hours.

3 Wash and dry the radicchio leaves thoroughly and lay them on individual plates.

4 Fish the chilli out of the dressing and discard. Taste and add pepper, if liked. Fill the salad leaves with the pasta just before serving.

I RISOTTI

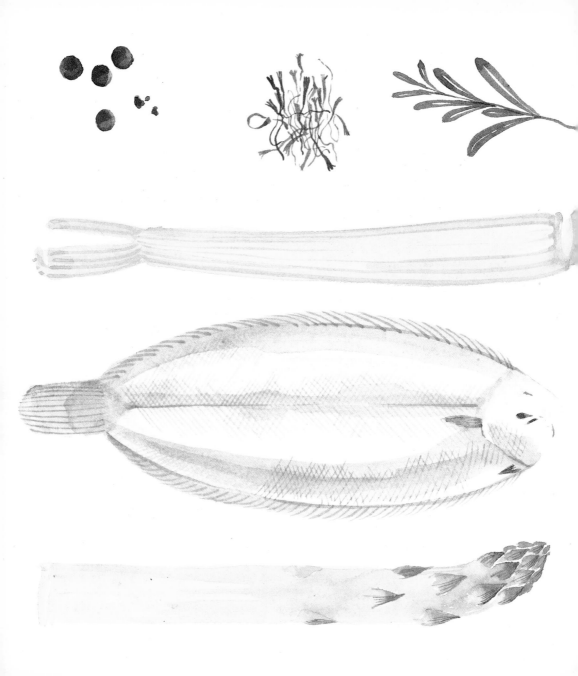

RISOTTI

Risotto is a relative newcomer to the Italian culinary scene, where most dishes can trace their origins back to the Renaissance, if not to Roman times. It was only during the nineteenth century that risotto became popular in the northern regions of Italy – Piedmont, Lombardy and Veneto – where the rice was cultivated, as indeed it still is.

A genuine risotto, for all its apparent simplicity, is a challenge to most cooks. Although there are certain rules to observe, the feel of making a good risotto can only be learnt with practice. The first essential is to use top quality ingredients. Secondly, one must remember that risotto is prepared according to a well-defined method. It is not just a mixture of rice and other ingredients, and it is certainly not, as some people have believed, a dish that Italians make from an assortment of leftovers. Rice is often the only ingredient, apart from flavourings. When there are other ingredients they are almost always cooked with the rice, so as to allow the flavours to combine and fuse.

The rice must be medium-grain white rice, which absorbs the liquid in which it cooks and which swells up without breaking or becoming mushy. Only two types of rice are suitable for making risotto: superfino and fino. Arborio, which is widely available, is the most popular variety of superfino rice and is suitable for all risotti. It has large plump grains with a delicious nutty taste when cooked. Carnaroli, a new superfino variety, is produced in relatively small quantities. It keeps its firm consistency, while its starch dissolves deliciously during the cooking. Vialone Nano, a fino rice, has a shorter, stubbier grain containing starch of a kind that does not soften easily in the cooking. It is my favourite rice for vegetable risotti. Vialone Nano cooks more quickly than

Arborio – 15 minutes as opposed to 20 minutes for Arborio. Both Carnaroli and Vialone Nano can be found in specialist Italian shops. In most of the recipes I have specified the best variety of rice to use, bearing in mind availability.

The choice of saucepan is crucial to the success of the dish. The pan must be wide, heavy-bottomed and large enough to contain the rice when it has finished cooking, by which time it will have increased its volume by nearly three times. Ideally it should also be round-bottomed, to prevent the rice from sticking in the corners.

The quality of the stock is also very important. It should be a good, but light, meat stock, made with a piece of veal, some beef, one or two pieces of chicken and very few bones, all flavoured with vegetables, herbs and seasonings. Pork and lamb are never used for this kind of stock. Vegetable stock is particularly suitable for a vegetable or fish risotto; for the latter a light fish stock is also good. If you have not got any stock already prepared, use good quality meat stock cubes; there are some on the market that do not contain monosodium glutamate.

Good quality Italian rice takes about 15–20 minutes to cook, according to the variety. At the end of the cooking the rice should be *al dente* – firm but tender without a chalky centre – and the risotto should have a creamy consistency.

You will find here recipes for 12 risotti, many with vegetables, others with fish and with meat. These last are more nourishing and are definitely main course dishes, while the lighter risotti with vegetables can be the start, *all'Italiana*, of any dinner party.

Risotto should be eaten as soon as it is done, but if you do not like to cook when your guests have already arrived, you can make a *timballo* instead, and accompany it with a suitable sauce if you wish. For this, keep the risotto slightly undercooked, being careful to add the stock very gradually at the end of the cooking or the rice will be too liquid when it is ready. Spread the risotto out on a large dish and leave it to cool. When it is cold, spoon it into a ring mould that has been generously buttered and sprinkled with dried breadcrumbs.

Set the mould in a bain-marie and bake in the oven heated to 220°C/425°F/Gas Mark 7 for about 20 minutes. Loosen the risotto all round the mould with a palette knife. Place a large round platter over it and turn the whole thing upside-down. Give the mould a few taps on the top, shake the platter and mould vigorously and lift the mould away. If some of the risotto sticks to the mould, remove it and patch the shape up neatly. Nobody will notice, especially if you place some basil or parsley over it.

RISOTTO AL LIMONE
RISOTTO WITH LEMON

Serves 4 as a first course or 3
as a main course

1.25l/2pt home-made light meat
stock or vegetable stock
60g/2oz unsalted butter
1 tbsp olive oil
2 shallots, very finely chopped
1 celery stick, very finely
chopped
300g/10oz Italian rice,
preferably Arborio
$\frac{1}{2}$ unwaxed lemon
5 or 6 fresh sage leaves
leaves from a small sprig of
fresh rosemary
1 egg yolk
4 tbsp freshly grated Parmesan
4 tbsp double cream
salt and freshly ground
black pepper

This recipe was in my book, *Secrets from an Italian Kitchen*. Friends and reviewers alike have all said they found it one of the best risotti ever, which is why I feel no qualms about repeating it here.

1 Bring the stock to a gentle simmer (keep it simmering all through the cooking of the rice).

2 Heat half the butter, the oil, shallots and celery in a heavy bottomed saucepan and sauté until the *soffritto* – frying mixture – of shallot and celery is softened (about 7 minutes). Mix in the rice and continue to sauté, stirring, until the rice is well coated with the fats and is partly translucent.

3 Pour over about 150ml/$\frac{1}{4}$pt of the simmering stock. Stir very thoroughly and cook until the rice has absorbed nearly all of the stock, still stirring. Add another ladleful of simmering stock, and continue in this manner until the rice is ready. You may not need all the stock. Good quality Italian rice for risotto takes 15–20 minutes to cook.

4 Meanwhile, thinly pare the zest from the lemon half and chop it with the herbs. Mix into the rice halfway through the cooking.

5 Squeeze the half lemon into a small bowl and combine it with the egg yolk, Parmesan, cream, a little salt and a very generous grinding of black pepper. Mix well with a fork.

6 When the rice is *al dente*, draw the pan off the heat and stir in the egg and cream mixture and the remaining butter. Cover the pan and leave to rest for 2 minutes or so. Then give the risotto an energetic stir, transfer to a heated dish or bowl and serve at once, with more grated Parmesan in a little bowl if you wish.

RISOTTO ALLA MILANESE

RISOTTO WITH SAFFRON

Serves 4–5 as a first course or
as an accompaniment

1.5l/2½pt home-made light
meat stock
1 small onion, very finely
chopped
75g/2½oz unsalted butter
350g/¾lb Italian rice, preferably
Carnaroli
180ml/6fl oz good red wine
½ tsp powdered saffron or saffron
strands crushed to a powder
salt and freshly ground
black pepper
75g/2½oz Parmesan,
freshly grated

Some Italians have queried the use of red wine instead of white in this recipe. My answer is that not only in my own family – Milanese for generations – but in some very authoritative books the wine suggested is red. Other recipes do not include any wine, but add some cream or milk at the end. The choice is yours.

As for the saffron, the strands are definitely more reliable than the powder, but they must be added earlier in the cooking so as to dissolve well, thus losing some flavour during the cooking.

This is the risotto traditionally served with Ossobuco and with Costolette alla Milanese, breaded veal cutlets.

1 Bring the stock to simmering point (keep it at a very low simmer all through the cooking of the rice).
2 Put the onion and 60g/2oz of the butter in a heavy-bottomed saucepan and sauté until soft and translucent. Add the rice and stir until well coated with fat. Sauté until the rice is partly translucent. Pour in the wine and boil for 1 minute, stirring constantly, and then pour in 150ml/¼pt of the simmering stock. Cook until nearly all the stock has been absorbed and then add another ladleful of the simmering stock. Continue cooking and adding small quantities of stock, while keeping the risotto at a steady lively simmer all the time. If you finish the stock before the rice is properly cooked, add a little boiling water.
3 About halfway through the cooking (good rice takes about 15–20 minutes to cook), add the saffron dissolved in a little stock. When the rice is *al dente*, taste and adjust the seasoning.
4 Draw the pan off the heat and mix in the rest of the butter and 4 tbsp of the Parmesan. Put the lid on and leave for 1 minute or

so. When the butter and the Parmesan have melted, give the risotto a vigorous stir and transfer to a heated dish. Serve immediately, with the rest of the cheese handed round separately.

RISOTTO AL POMODORO
RISOTTO WITH TOMATOES

The match of risotto with tomatoes is a modern one, but it is so good that I am sure it will become a classic. This risotto does not contain any butter. It is very light and fresh, and it is very good, if not better, cold.

1 Cut the peeled tomatoes in half. Squeeze out and discard some of the seeds. Chop the tomatoes coarsely and put them in a heavy-bottomed saucepan large enough to hold the rice later. Remember that the rice will be nearly three times its original volume by the end of the cooking.

2 Add 4 tbsp of the oil to the pan, then add the garlic and half the basil. Cook briskly for 1–2 minutes, stirring.

3 Meanwhile, bring the stock to a simmer (keep it simmering very gently all through the making of the risotto).

4 Add the rice to the pan with the tomatoes and cook for about 2 minutes, stirring constantly.

5 Pour over a ladleful of simmering stock and continue cooking, adding more stock little by little until the rice is *al dente*. If you want to serve the risotto cold, remove it from the heat when the rice is slightly underdone; it finishes cooking as it cools.

6 Add salt and pepper to taste and mix in the rest of the oil. Transfer to a serving dish and sprinkle the remaining basil leaves on the top. If you serve the risotto cold, fluff it up with a fork before bringing it to the table.

Serves 4 as a first course or 3 as a main course

700g/1½lb ripe tomatoes, peeled
7 tbsp extra virgin olive oil
3 or 4 garlic cloves, thickly sliced
a good handful of fresh basil leaves, torn into pieces
1.25l/2pt vegetable stock
300g/10oz Italian rice, preferably Carnaroli
salt and freshly ground black pepper

RISOTTO AL FINOCCHIO

RISOTTO WITH FENNEL

Serves 4–5 as a first course or
3–4 as a main course

2 fennel bulbs, about 600g/1¼lb
1 tbsp olive oil
60g/2oz unsalted butter
1 small onion, finely chopped
1 celery stick, finely chopped
1.25l/2pt vegetable stock
salt and freshly ground
black pepper
300g/10oz Italian rice,
preferably Vialone Nano
6 tbsp dry white wine
4 tbsp double cream
50g/1¾oz Parmesan,
freshly grated

Vegetable risotti are one of the great strengths of Venetian cooking. Of all of them, this fennel risotto is my favourite, especially when I can get hold of fennel that is full of flavour and not 'the commercial variety grown in Italy for export which is beautiful but dumb' as the late Jane Grigson so aptly put it in her splendid *Vegetable Book*.

1 Cut off and discard the fennel stalks, but keep some of the feathery green foliage. Remove any bruised outer leaves and then cut the bulbs lengthwise in half. Slice the halves very finely across. Wash thoroughly and drain.

2 Put the oil, half the butter, the onion and celery in a smallish sauté pan. Sauté until the vegetables are pale gold. Add the sliced fennel and stir it over and over to let it take up the flavour. Add about 4 tbsp of the stock and cover the pan. Cook, stirring occasionally, for about 20 minutes or until the fennel is very soft. Mash it with a fork to a purée over high heat, so that the excess liquid evaporates. Add salt to taste.

3 Bring the remaining stock to a gentle simmer (keep it simmering all through the cooking of the rice).

4 Heat the remaining butter in a heavy-bottomed saucepan. When the butter foam begins to subside, mix in the rice and stir to coat the grains thoroughly. Sauté for a couple of minutes until the rice is partly translucent. Turn the heat up and add the wine. Let it bubble away, stirring the rice constantly.

5 Now begin to add the simmering stock a ladleful at a time. When nearly all of the first ladleful has been absorbed, add another, always stirring the rice. If you run out of stock before the rice is done, add some boiling water and continue the cooking.

6 Halfway through the cooking of the rice, stir in the mashed fennel with all the cooking juices.

7 When the rice is *al dente*, draw the pan from the heat and add the cream, Parmesan and a generous grinding of pepper. Mix everything well together. Transfer to a heated dish, scatter the reserved fennel foliage, previously snipped, over the top and serve at once.

RISOTTO AL PEPERONE
RISOTTO WITH PEPPERS

Serves 4 as a first course or 3
as a main course

6 tbsp extra virgin olive oil
2 garlic cloves, sliced
3 tbsp chopped fresh parsley
4 tomatoes, peeled, seeded
and chopped
2 large peppers, preferably
1 yellow and 1 red
1.25l/2pt vegetable stock
300g/10oz Italian rice,
preferably Arborio or
Vialone Nano
4 pinches of chilli powder
salt and freshly ground
black pepper
12 fresh basil leaves

Risotto, the staple of northern Italy, used never to be made with olive oil, the cooking fat of the south. But a few modern risotti are now very successfully made with oil, and with ingredients, in this case peppers, whose ideal dressing is oil.

This is my adaptation of a traditional risotto from Voghera, a town in south-west Lombardy that is famous for its peppers.

1 Heat 4 tbsp of the oil in a heavy-bottomed saucepan with the garlic and parsley. When the garlic and parsley begin to sizzle, add the chopped tomatoes and cook for 5 minutes, stirring frequently.

2 Meanwhile wash and dry the peppers. Peel them, using a swivel-headed vegetable peeler. You should 'saw' from side to side with it as you peel, rather than sliding it straight down the pepper. If you find them difficult to peel, leave the skin on. Discard the cores, seeds and white ribs, and cut the peppers into small cubes.

3 Add the peppers to the pan and cook for 10 minutes, stirring frequently.

4 Meanwhile, bring the stock to a simmer in another pan. (Keep it just simmering all through the cooking). Add the rice to the tomato and pepper mixture and stir very well, letting it absorb the juices. After about 1–2 minutes, begin to add the simmering stock by the ladleful. Wait to add each subsequent ladleful until the previous one has nearly all been absorbed.

5 When the rice is *al dente*, about 18 minutes, add the chilli powder and salt and pepper to taste. Draw the pan off the heat and stir in the remaining 2 tbsp of oil. Transfer to a heated deep serving dish, sprinkle with the basil leaves and serve at once.

RISOTTO ALLA PAESANA
RISOTTO WITH VEGETABLES

This lovely fresh risotto is best made in the spring, when the new peas and asparagus are in season. The vegetables can be varied: you can put in a little celery and carrot when there is no asparagus; French beans are suitable too. Try to match the flavours of the vegetables so as not to have a strident note.

1 Cook the fresh peas in lightly salted boiling water until just tender. Meanwhile, trim and wash the asparagus and cook them in boiling salted water until *al dente*. Drain and cut the tender part of the spears into small pieces. (Reserve the rest for a soup or a mousse.) Blanch the courgette for 2–3 minutes, then drain and cut into small cubes. Cut the tomatoes in half, squeeze out the seeds and then cut into short strips.

2 Put half the oil, the parsley and garlic in a sauté pan and sauté for 1 minute. Stir in all the vegetables, season lightly with salt and sauté over low heat for 2 minutes for them to take the flavour of the *soffritto* – the fried mixture. Set aside.

3 Heat the stock in a saucepan until just simmering (keep it simmering all through the cooking of the rice).

4 Put the rest of the oil and half the butter in a heavy-bottomed saucepan. Add the shallots and sauté until tender. Add the rice and stir to coat with the fats, then cook for 2 minutes or until partly translucent. Splash with the wine and boil rapidly to evaporate, stirring constantly. Add a ladleful of simmering stock and let the rice absorb it while you stir constantly. Continue to add the stock gradually, stirring frequently, until the rice is *al dente*. (This will take about 15 to 20 minutes, according to the quality of the rice.)

5 Halfway through the cooking, stir in the vegetables with all their cooking juices. Season with pepper; taste to check the salt.

Serves 4 as a first course or 3 as a main course

100g/3½oz podded fresh peas
225g/½lb asparagus
100g/3½oz courgette
225g/½lb ripe firm tomatoes, peeled, Italian canned or plum tomatoes, drained
4 tbsp extra virgin olive oil
a bunch of fresh parsley, chopped
1 garlic clove, chopped
salt and freshly ground black pepper
1.25l/2pt chicken or vegetable stock
30g/1oz unsalted butter
2 shallots, chopped
250g/9oz Italian rice, preferably Vialone Nano
5 tbsp dry white wine
45g/1½oz Parmesan, freshly grated
12 fresh basil leaves, torn into pieces

6 When the rice is done, draw the pan off the heat and add the rest of the butter, cut into small pieces, and the Parmesan. Place the lid tightly on the pan and allow to stand for a couple of minutes. Then stir vigorously and transfer to a heated dish. Garnish with the basil leaves and serve at once.

RISOTTO COI PEOCI
RISOTTO WITH MUSSELS

Serves 4 as a first course or 3 as a main course

1.8kg/4lb mussels
300ml/½pt dry white wine
4 tbsp chopped fresh parsley, preferably flat-leaf
6 tbsp olive oil
3 shallots or 1 medium onion, very finely chopped
salt and freshly ground black pepper
1l/1¾pt light fish or vegetable stock
1 celery stick, with the leaves if possible
1 garlic clove
½ dried chilli, crumbled
300g/10oz Italian rice, preferably Arborio or Vialone Nano

I have always found a risotto with mussels to be rather unsatisfactory, because you either have only risotto in your mouth, albeit fish tasting, or else a large mussel. So one day I came up with the idea of chopping up most of the mussels so that morsels of them could be enjoyed in each mouthful. This is the recipe I developed and it works very well.

1 First clean the mussels. Scrape off the barnacles, tug off the beard and scrub thoroughly with a stiff brush under running water. Throw away any mussel that remains open after you have tapped it on a hard surface; this means it's dead.
2 Put the wine in a large sauté pan, add the mussels and cover the pan. Cook over high heat until the mussels are open, which will only take 3–4 minutes. Shake the pan every now and then.
3 As soon as the mussels are open, remove the meat from the shells and discard the shells. Strain the cooking liquid through a sieve lined with muslin, pouring it slowly and gently so that the sand will be left at the bottom of the pan.
4 Set aside a dozen of the nicest mussels; chop the rest and put in a bowl. Mix in the parsley.

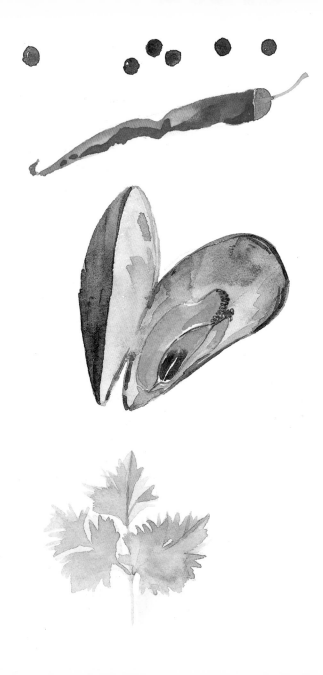

5 Pour the oil into a heavy-bottomed saucepan. Add the shallots or onion and a pinch of salt and sauté until the shallot is soft and just beginning to colour.

6 In another saucepan, heat the stock to simmering point (keep it just simmering all through the cooking of the rice).

7 Meanwhile, chop the celery and garlic together. Add to the shallot with the chilli. Sauté for a further minute or so. Now add the rice and stir to coat with oil, then cook it for a couple of minutes until partly translucent. Pour over the mussel liquid and stir well. When the liquid has been absorbed add the simmering stock, one ladleful at a time. Stir constantly at first. When the rice is nearly cooked, mix in the chopped mussels, then continue cooking until *al dente*.

8 Season with salt, if necessary, and pepper. Transfer to a heated dish and garnish with the reserved whole mussels.

RISOTTO CON LE ANIMELLE

RISOTTO WITH SWEETBREADS

In restaurants, sweetbreads are often accompanied by boiled rice. That rather boring presentation has, however, led me to devise this dish, where the winey-syrupy sweetbreads are combined with a classic *risotto in bianco*.

During the truffle season a small white truffle shaved over the top of the risotto makes the dish truly sensational.

1 Soak the sweetbreads in cold water for at least 1 hour. Rinse them and put them in a pan with half lemon and 1 tsp of salt. Cover with fresh cold water and bring to the boil. Boil for 2 minutes. Drain well, plunge into cold water and drain again.

Remove all fat and the white tubes, as well as the hard bits. Put the sweetbreads between two plates with a weight on top to squeeze out all excess liquid. Dry them and cut them into morsels.

2 Heat the stock to simmering (keep it simmering all through the cooking of the risotto).

3 Melt half the butter in a heavy-bottomed saucepan. Add the shallots, 4 of the sage leaves and a pinch of salt and cook until the shallots are soft and translucent.

4 Add the rice and stir to coat with butter, then sauté for 2 to 3 minutes until partly translucent. Pour in the wine and boil for a minute or two until it has evaporated, stirring constantly. Now begin to add simmering stock, little by little, in the usual way. Do not add too much at one time or the risotto will not cook properly. Keep the heat lively and constant.

5 Meanwhile, melt half the remaining butter in a sauté or frying pan. Add the rest of the sage leaves. When the sage begins to sizzle, slide in the sweetbreads and sauté for 2 minutes, turning them over to brown on all sides. Add the Marsala to the pan and let it bubble away on a slow heat. Cook for 7–8 minutes, stirring occasionally.

6 When the rice is nearly done, pour the sweetbreads and all the juices into the risotto pan. Stir thoroughly. Taste and adjust the seasoning, and finish cooking the risotto.

7 When the rice is *al dente*, draw the pan off the heat. Add the remaining butter and a couple of spoonsful of the Parmesan. Cover the pan tightly and let the butter melt for a minute or so, then stir the risotto gently but thoroughly. Transfer to a heated dish and serve at once, handing round the rest of the Parmesan in a bowl.

Serves 4 as a main course

450g/1lb lamb sweetbreads
½ lemon
salt and freshly ground black pepper
1.25l/2pt light meat stock
120g/4oz unsalted butter
2 shallots, finely chopped
about 8 fresh sage leaves, snipped
300g/10oz Italian rice, preferably Arborio
6 tbsp dry white wine
4 tbsp Marsala (Madeira or port can also be used)
75g/2½oz Parmesan, freshly grated

RISOTTO CON LE SOGLIOLE

RISOTTO WITH DOVER SOLE

Serves 4 as a main course

75g/2½oz unsalted butter
2 tbsp very finely chopped
shallot
salt and freshly ground
black pepper
1.25l/2pt light fish stock
350g/¾lb Italian rice,
preferably Carnaroli
120ml/4fl oz dry white wine
2 tbsp chopped fresh dill
350g/¾lb skinless Dover
sole fillets
4 tbsp freshly grated Parmesan

It might seem extravagant to use Dover sole in a humble dish such as a risotto, but I assure you that it is necessary. You only need a small amount of Dover sole, and it does make a great difference to the dish. The delicacy and firm texture of the fish is in perfect harmony with the soft creaminess of the risotto; none of the other ingredients disturbs this happy balance of flavours.

1 Heat 60g/2oz of the butter and the shallot in a heavy-bottomed saucepan. Add a pinch of salt and sauté until the shallot is soft and translucent.

2 Meanwhile, heat the fish stock in another saucepan to simmering (keep it at the lowest simmer all through the cooking of the risotto).

3 Add the rice to the shallot and stir to coat with butter, then sauté for a minute or so until partly translucent. Splash with wine and let it bubble away, stirring constantly.

4 Add about 150ml/¼pt of simmering stock, stir well and let the rice absorb the liquid. Continue adding stock little by little until the rice is nearly done, then mix in half of the dill and continue the cooking.

5 Meanwhile, heat the remaining butter in a non-stick frying pan. Cut the fish fillets in half, across. Slide them into the butter and sauté for 3 minutes. Turn them over and sauté for a further minute. Sprinkle with salt and pepper.

6 When the rice is *al dente*, mix in the Parmesan and the juices from the fish fillets. Turn into a heated dish. Place the fish fillets neatly over the top and sprinkle with the remaining dill. Serve immediately.

RISOTTO ALLA SCOZZESE
RISOTTO WITH SMOKED SALMON AND
WHISKY

Serves 4 as a first course or 3
as a main course

60g/2oz unsalted butter
4 tbsp finely chopped shallot
salt
1.25l/2 pt vegetable or light
chicken stock
300g/10oz Italian rice,
preferably Carnaroli
4 tbsp Scotch whisky
225g/$\frac{1}{2}$lb smoked salmon,
cut into 2cm/$\frac{3}{4}$in pieces
5 tbsp double cream
2 tbsp chopped fresh dill
cayenne pepper
freshly grated Parmesan,
to serve

I love smoked salmon and, like most Italians, am not averse to an occasional glass of whisky. So here I have combined these two very Scottish ingredients with a favourite dish from my home country. This match with a Lombard risotto is particularly successful. The Parmesan is not necessary, but I think its flavour goes well with that of the smoked salmon.

1 Put the butter in a large, heavy-bottomed saucepan. Add the chopped shallot and a pinch of salt; this will release the moisture from the shallot thus preventing it from browning. Sauté until soft and translucent, about 7 minutes.

2 Meanwhile, in another saucepan heat the stock to simmering point (keep it simmering all through the cooking of the rice).

3 Add the rice to the shallot and stir to coat with butter, then cook for a couple of minutes, stirring constantly, until partly translucent. Add the whisky and let it bubble away, stirring constantly. Add a ladleful of simmering stock and cook the rice on a lively heat, adding a ladleful of stock whenever the rice begins to get dry.

4 When the rice is *al dente*, add the smoked salmon, cream, dill and cayenne pepper to taste. Mix thoroughly and check the salt before you transfer this delicious risotto to a heated dish. Serve at once, handing the cheese separately in a bowl for those who want it.

RISOTTO CON LA SALSICCIA
RISOTTO WITH SAUSAGE

Some recipes for this dish, originally from Monza (now a suburb of Milan) suggest cutting the sausage in chunks and cooking it separately. In this case the sausage is also served separately and is added to the risotto by each diner. I find this version more suitable if I am serving the risotto as a main course. Here, however, the recipe is for a real risotto, the sausage being added to the rice about 10 minutes before the rice is ready, so that the flavours of the two ingredients will blend thoroughly.

You need good 100% pure pork sausage.

---

1 Skin the sausage and crumble it. Heat 1 tbsp of oil and the sage in a non-stick frying pan. Add the sausage and fry briskly for 5 minutes, stirring constantly. Pour over the wine, bring to the boil and cook for about 5 minutes, only enough for the sausage meat to lose its raw colour.

2 While the sausage is cooking bring the stock to a simmer (keep it just simmering all through the cooking of the rice).

3 Heat butter and remaining oil in a heavy-bottomed saucepan. Add the shallots and fry gently until soft and translucent – about 7 minutes.

4 Add the rice to the shallot *soffritto* and cook for 1–2 minutes, stirring constantly, until the grains are partly translucent.

5 Add the simmering stock a ladleful at a time. Wait to add another ladleful until the previous one has nearly all been absorbed.

6 Ten minutes after you start adding the stock, add the sausage and its juice to the rice. Stir well and continue cooking until the rice is *al dente*. Check the seasoning and serve at once, with the Parmesan handed round separately if you wish.

Serves 4 as a first course or 3 as a main course

350g/¾lb luganega sausage or other pure pork, coarse-grained, continental sausage
2 tbsp olive oil
1 sprig of fresh sage
150ml/¼pt full-bodied red wine, such as Barbera
1.25l/2pt light meat stock
45g/1½oz unsalted butter
2 or 3 shallots, depending on size, finely chopped
300g/10oz Italian rice, preferably Arborio or Carnaroli
salt and freshly ground black pepper
freshly grated Parmesan, to serve (optional)

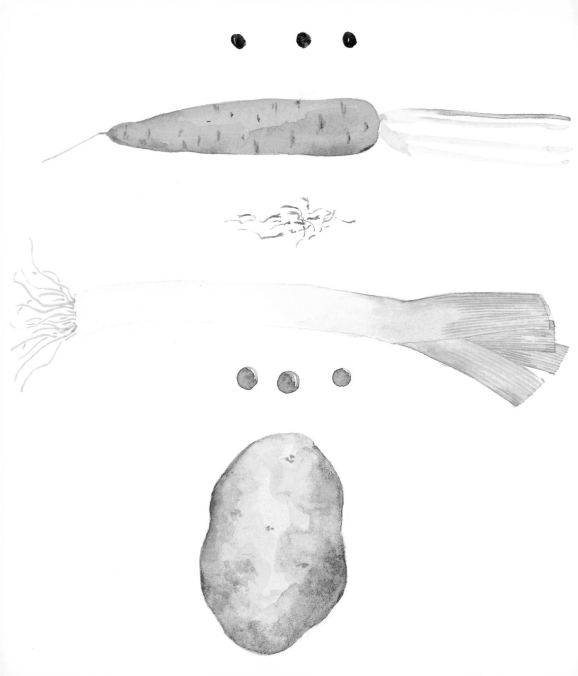

TIMBALLI E PASTICCI DI RISO

MOULDED AND BAKED RICE DISHES

I have included three recipes for this type of rice preparation. There are two elegant moulded dishes and a rice, potato and mussel pie of peasant origin but of great gastronomic merit. All three are particularly suited to dinner parties, since they can be made in advance and then baked in the oven. They are dishes that need a more experienced cook, able to judge the exact cooking time of the different ingredients, and, in the case of the moulded dishes, able to shape and unmould the rice. A good point, however, is that cooked rice is very malleable. Should you find yourself with a timballo *tombé*, you can reshape the rice with your hands and nobody will know. The pie is easy as regards presentation, but requires knowledge in the timing.

SFORMATO DI RISOTTO E PORRI CON LA SALSA DI COZZE

MOULDED LEEK RISOTTO WITH MUSSEL
SAUCE

Serves 6 as a first course or 4 as a main course

1kg/2¼lb mussels
1 tbsp olive oil
2 garlic cloves
1 thick slice of lemon
350g/¾lb leeks
1.25/2pt vegetable stock
120g/4oz unsalted butter
450g/1lb Italian rice, preferably Vialone Nano
300ml/½pt dry white wine
salt and freshly ground black pepper
dried breadcrumbs for the mould
1 shallot, finely chopped
¼ tsp saffron strands
2 tsp cornflour

Leeks and mussels are complementary flavours. The rice here unites them and gives substance to this lovely dish.

1 Scrub the mussels in cold water, knock off the barncles and tug off the beard. Rinse in several changes of cold water. Discard any mussel that remains open after you have tapped it against a hard surface.

2 Put the oil, garlic and slice of lemon in a large sauté pan. Add the mussels, cover the pan and cook over high heat until the mussels are open, about 4 minutes. Shake the pan very often.

3 Remove the mussel meat from the shells and discard the shells. Filter the liquid through a sieve lined with muslin. Set aside.

4 Cut off the green part of the leeks. Choose the best green leaves, wash them and blanch in boiling water for 2–3 minutes. Drain and cut into 1cm/½in strips. Set aside.

5 Cut the white part of the leeks into very thin pieces. Wash thoroughly, drain and dry them.

6 Heat the stock in a saucepan until simmering (keep it simmering all through the making of the risotto).

7 Heat the oven to 180°C/350°F/Gas Mark 4.

8 Heat 60g/2oz of the butter and the white part of the leeks in a large heavy-bottomed saucepan. Sauté until the leeks are just soft and then mix in the rice. Sauté the rice until it is well coated with butter and the grains are partly translucent – about 2 minutes – and then pour over half the wine. Boil briskly for 1 minute, stirring constantly.

9 Add a ladleful of the simmering stock and stir well. As soon as nearly all the stock has been absorbed, add another ladleful of stock. Continue cooking the rice in this manner until it is very *al dente*, about 15 minutes. Mix in 30g/1oz of the butter. Taste and check the seasoning.

10 Very generously butter a 1.5l/2½pt cake tin, mould or soufflé dish and coat it with breadcrumbs. Spoon the risotto into it, press down gently and place in the oven while you prepare the sauce.

11 Put the shallot and remaining butter in a saucepan and sauté for 5 minutes.

12 Meanwhile, pound the saffron in a mortar. Add 2–3 tbsp of the mussel liquid and stir thoroughly. Add the cornflour and stir hard until amalgamated. Pour the mixture into the shallot pan and add the remaining wine and mussel liquid. Bring to the boil very slowly, stirring constantly. Allow to simmer for a few minutes for the sauce to thicken and then add the mussels. Add salt and pepper to taste. Cover the pan and draw off the heat.

13 Loosen the risotto from the mould with a palette knife. Turn the mould over onto a heated round platter. Tap and shake the mould and then lift it off. Drape the strips of the green part of the leeks over the risotto at regular intervals. Spoon a little of the mussel sauce over the top and pour the rest into a heated bowl. Serve immediately.

ANELLO DI RISOTTO COI FEGATINI E I FUNGHI

RISOTTO RING WITH CHICKEN LIVERS
AND DRIED PORCINI

Serves 6 as a first course or
4–5 as a main course

For the sauce

30g/1oz dried porcini
30g/1oz unsalted butter
150g/5oz fresh chicken livers
60g/2oz fresh Italian sausage
such as luganega, or Toulouse
sausage, skinned
200g/7oz skinned and boned
chicken breast, cut into
bite-size pieces
100/3½oz podded fresh young
peas, or frozen petits pois
2 pinches of ground cloves
120ml/4fl oz red wine
salt and freshly ground
black pepper

The plain risotto is served in a ring, the centre of which is filled with a rich sauce. It is a showy dish for a dinner party.

1 Soak the dried porcini in very hot water for 30 minutes. Lift them out, rinse them and dry them. Chop them coarsely. Filter the porcini liquid through a sieve lined with muslin.
2 Heat the butter in a small saucepan. Add the porcini and cook gently for about 10 minutes.

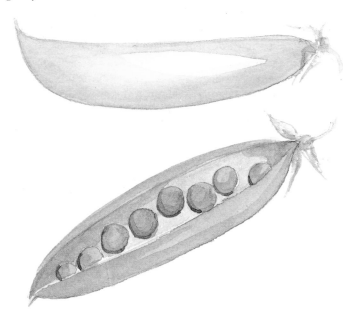

3 Meanwhile, clean the chicken livers, removing all the fat and gristle. Cut into bite-size pieces and put in a small saucepan with the sausage, chicken and peas. Add the cloves, wine, and salt and pepper to taste. Bring to the boil and cook, uncovered, for about 10 minutes, stirring very frequently. Mix in the porcini with all their juices and continue cooking for a further 10 minutes. Taste to check the seasoning. Set aside, and reheat before serving.

4 To make the risotto, first bring the stock to a simmer (keep it just simmering all through the cooking of the rice).

5 Heat half the butter with the onion, celery and carrot in a wide heavy-bottomed saucepan. Cook gently until the vegetables are soft, about 10 minutes, stirring very frequently.

6 Heat the oven to 170°C/325°F/Gas Mark 3.

7 Mix the rice into the vegetables and sauté for a minute or so until the grains are partly translucent. Stir in the tomato purée, cook for $\frac{1}{2}$ minute and then pour in the wine. Boil rapidly for 1 minute, stirring constantly.

8 Add a ladleful of the simmering stock and 2–3 tbsp of the porcini liquid. Cook the risotto, gradually adding the remaining stock in the usual way. When the risotto is nearly done and still on the liquid side, draw off the heat. Taste and add salt and pepper. Mix in the rest of the butter and the Parmesan. Cover the pan and leave until the butter has melted, and then mix thoroughly.

9 Meanwhile, generously butter a 1 l/1¾pt ring mould. Coat with breadcrumbs, shaking out excess crumbs.

10 Spoon the risotto into the mould. Place the mould in the oven and heat for about 10 minutes.

11 Turn the risotto out onto a heated round platter and spoon the hot sauce into the hole.

For the risotto
60g/2oz unsalted butter
2 tbsp finely chopped onion
1 tbsp finely chopped celery
1 tbsp finely chopped carrot
400g/14oz Italian rice, preferably Vialone Nano
1 tbsp tomato purée
120ml/4fl oz red wine
1.5l/2½pt chicken stock
salt and freshly ground black pepper
6 tbsp freshly grated Parmesan
butter and dried breadcrumbs for the mould

PATATE, RISO E COZZE DI PIETRO
—————— POTATO, RICE AND MUSSEL PIE ——————

Serves 4 as a main course

2kg/4½lb mussels
180ml/6fl oz dry white wine
700g/1½lb waxy potatoes
5 tbsp chopped fresh flat-leaf
parsley
3 tsp dried oregano
7 tbsp extra virgin olive oil
1 garlic clove, sliced
salt and freshly ground
black pepper
180g/6½oz Italian rice,
preferably Vialone Nano
1 large courgette, sliced
200g/7oz Italian or Spanish
onion, very finely sliced
5 tbsp grated aged pecorino
400g/14oz Italian canned
chopped tomatoes

My friend Pietro Pesce is a serious connoisseur of good food. Being a Venetian, he is also a great champion of northern Italian cooking, so that when he came back from Bari, in the south, and gave me this recipe I was quite sure it was worth testing.

The original recipe advises one not to add the mussel juices to the pie because it would make the dish too salty. But when I tested it with Atlantic mussels, less salty and less flavourful, I decided to add the juices to give the pie the necessary taste of fish and the sea.

————————

1 Scrub the mussels in cold water, knock off the barnacles and tug off the beard. Rinse in several changes of cold water until there is no sand at the bottom of the sink. Throw away any mussel which is open and remains open after you tap it on a hard surface. It is dead. Set aside a dozen of the best-looking mussels.

2 Put the wine and the remaining mussels in a large sauté pan. Cook, covered, until the mussels open – about 4 minutes. Shake the pan frequently. Remove the mussels as they open, or they will toughen. Eventually all the shells containing a mussel will indeed open.

3 Take the meat out of the shells and discard the shells. Filter the mussel liquid through a sieve lined with a piece of muslin. You will have about 600ml/1pt of liquid. Set the meat and the liquid aside in separate bowls.

4 Scrub and wash again the shells of the unshelled mussels and set aside.

5 Peel the potatoes and cut them into wafer-thin slices. I use a food processor fitted with the fine blade disc. Put the potatoes in a bowl and toss them with 1 tbsp of parsley, 1 tsp of oregano, 2 tbsp of the oil, a sliver or two of garlic and a good grinding of pepper.

6 Put the rice in another bowl and the courgette in a third bowl. Dress each of them with 1 tbsp of the oil, 1 tbsp of parsley, 1 tsp oregano, a sliver or two of garlic and a grinding of pepper.

7 Heat the oven to 180°C/350°F/Gas Mark 4.

8 Choose a shallow metal oven dish no more than 5cm/2in deep. Grease it well with some of the remaining oil.

9 Spread the onion over the bottom of the dish and cover with the courgette. Make a layer of half the potatoes and lay all the mussels, shelled and unshelled, over them. Pour about half the mussel liquid into the dish and sprinkle with two-thirds of the cheese. Level down with your hands, then add the rice and cover with the rest of the potatoes. Pour over the rest of the mussel liquid and season with lots of pepper.

10 Spread the tomatoes with all their juice all over the top and add enough boiling water to come nearly level with the top of the pie. Sprinkle with the remaining cheese and parsley and 1 tsp of salt. (Only a little salt is added because the mussel juices and the pecorino should have already salted the dish enough.) Drizzle the rest of the oil all over the pie.

11 Cover the pie with foil and bake for 1 hour. Remove the foil and continue baking until the potatoes are tender, which depends on their quality and on how thin the slices are. Remove from the oven and set the pie aside to rest for 10 minutes before serving, to allow the flavours to blend.

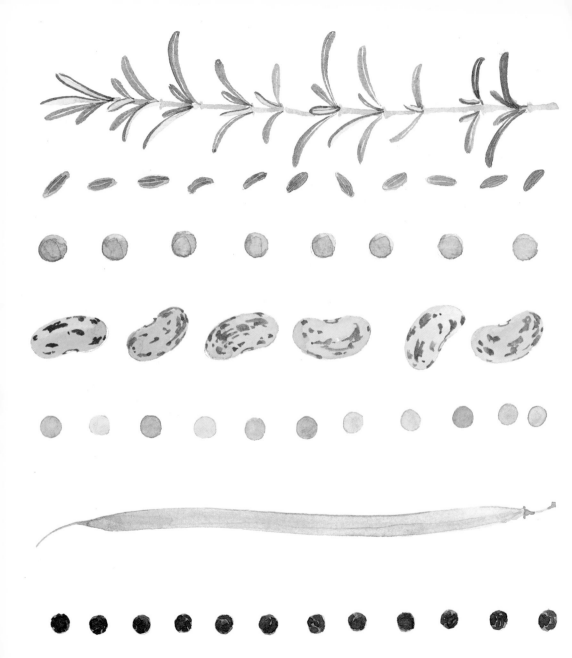

RISI ASCIUTTI E MINESTRE DI RISO

—— RICE AND VEGETABLE DISHES AND RICE SOUPS ——

The first two recipes in this section are for dishes that are midway between a soup and a risotto. The rice is boiled in the stock in which the vegetables are cooking, thus the dishes are definitely not risotti. This method of cooking ensures that the taste of the vegetable predominates over the flavour of the rice.

The last three recipes are for soups, all from my home town, Milan, the motherland of good soups. There, most families start their supper with a soup. Often it is a rice soup, which can vary from a rich earthy minestrone to a sophisticated soup with pieces of chicken and grains of rice and almonds floating in a pale blond pool – a very Chinese looking soup.

RISI E BISI

RICE WITH PEAS

Serves 4–6 as a first course

1 small onion, very finely chopped
45g/1½oz unsalted butter
1 tbsp olive oil
700g/1½lb young fresh peas, podded
1.5l/2½pt light meat stock
250g/9oz Italian rice, preferably Vialone Nano
1 tsp fennel seeds, crushed, or 2 tbsp chopped fresh flat-leaf parsley
75g/2½oz Parmesan, freshly grated
salt and freshly ground black pepper

The Venetians' love of rice and peas is sublimated in this, the most aristocratic of rice dishes. It was served at the Doge's banquets on the feast of San Marco, 25th April, when the first young peas, grown on the islands of the Venetian lagoon, appear in the market.

This is the old recipe, in which fennel seeds are used instead of parsley. The best rice for the dish is Vialone Nano.

1 Put the onion, half the butter and the oil in a heavy-bottomed saucepan and sauté until the onion is pale golden and soft. Mix in the peas and cook over low heat for 10 minutes, adding a few spoonsful of stock during the cooking.

2 Meanwhile, bring the remaining stock to the boil in another saucepan.

3 Add the rice to the peas and sauté for 2 minutes, turning the rice over and over until the grains are partly translucent. Now pour over the boiling stock. Stir well and bring back to the boil. Simmer gently, stirring occasionally, until the rice is *al dente*. You might have to add a little more stock during the cooking.

4 A few minutes before the rice is done, add the fennel seeds or parsley, the rest of the butter and 4 tbsp of Parmesan. Taste and add salt and pepper to your liking. Stir thoroughly and finish the cooking, then serve at once with rest of the cheese handed round separately.

RISO E LENTICCHIE
─── RICE WITH LENTILS ───

This is an earthy, nourishing soup which I first had one lunchtime in Rome in a busy, bustling trattoria opposite the Quirinale. It was the most lively place imaginable, crowded with civil servants enjoying good homely Roman food.

─────────

1 Heat the oil, onion and pancetta in a heavy-bottomed saucepan. (I use an earthenware pot when I cook pulses.) Sauté for about 7 minutes, stirring frequently. The onion must become soft but not coloured.

2 Chop together finely the carrot, celery, rosemary leaves and garlic. Add to the onion *soffritto* – frying mixture – and cook at low heat for about 10 minutes. Stir frequently. Season with salt and stir in the tomato purée. Cook for a further minute.

3 Meanwhile, heat the stock in a separate saucepan.

4 Add the lentils to the vegetable mixture. Stir well and let them *insaporire* – take up the flavour – for a minute or two.

5 Pour enough stock into the pan to cover the lentils by about 5cm/2in. Place a lid over the saucepan and cook until the lentils are soft, not *al dente*. It is difficult to say how long that will take since it depends on the quality and freshness of the pulses. Usually lentils are ready within 1 hour. Check the liquid every now and then and add more stock whenever the lentils are too dry.

6 Add the rest of the stock and bring back to the boil. Mix in the rice and, if necessary, add more boiling stock. If you have used all the stock, pour in boiling water. The amount of liquid needed varies with the quality of the lentils, the kind of rice used and the heat on which the soup is cooked. The resulting soup should be quite thick: lots of rice and lentils in a little liquid.

Serves 4–5

4 tbsp olive oil
1 small onion, very finely chopped
60g/2oz smoked pancetta, cut into tiny pieces
1 small carrot
1 large celery stick
1 sprig of fresh rosemary, about 5cm/2in long
1 garlic clove
salt and freshly ground black pepper
1 heaped tsp tomato purée
1.5l/2½pt vegetable stock or 2 vegetable stock cubes dissolved in the same amount of water
200g/7oz green lentils, rinsed and drained
200g/7oz Italian rice, preferably Vialone Nano
extra virgin olive oil for the table, a Tuscan or Roman oil

7 Season with lots of pepper, and simmer until the rice is *al dente* (15–20 minutes).

8 Taste and adjust the seasoning. Serve the soup straight away, handing round a bottle of extra virgin olive oil for everyone to pour a little over his serving of soup. Although not essential, I recommend this last *battesimo* – christening – because the oil livens up the earthy soup with its fruity flavour.

RISO CON LE VERDURE
RICE WITH VEGETABLES

Northern and southern Italy meet happily in this dish, which was given to me by the Neapolitan owner of a superb greengrocer in Valtellina, an Alpine valley north of Milan. The dish is halfway between a minestrone and a risotto with vegetables and yet it tastes different from either. The flavour of the vegetables comes through strongly, enhanced by the final *soffritto*.

1 Choose a large pot – I use my earthenware stockpot of 5l/8¾pt capacity. Put all the washed and cut vegetables in it and add enough water to come three-quarters of the way up the side of the pot. Season with salt, bring to the boil and simmer, uncovered, for 45 minutes.

2 Add the rice to the vegetables, stir well and cook for about 15 minutes or until done. The vegetables should be nice and soft and the rice should be *al dente*, thus giving a pleasing contrast of texture.

3 While the rice is cooking, make a little *soffritto* (frying mixture). Heat the oil, garlic and sage in a small frying pan until the sage begins to sizzle and the aroma of the garlic to rise. Add the tomatoes and cook for 5 minutes, stirring occasionally.

4 When the rice is ready, drain the contents of the stockpot very well (you can keep the liquid for a soup) and transfer the rice and vegetable mixture, a ladleful at a time, into a serving bowl. Dress each ladleful with a couple of spoonfuls of the *soffritto*, a handful of cheese cubes, a generous grinding of pepper and a spoonful of Parmesan. Mix very thoroughly after each addition, and serve at once.

Note: By dressing the dish gradually you make sure that the *soffritto* and the cheese are equally distributed.

Serves 6 as a first course or 4 as a main course

1 large waxy potato, diced
2 carrots, diced
1 large leek, white and green part, cut into rounds
120g/4oz podded fresh peas or green beans, according to season
1 celery stalk, stringed and diced
1 courgette, diced
salt and freshly ground black pepper
300g/10oz Italian rice, preferably Vialone Nano
100ml/3½fl oz extra virgin olive oil
3 garlic cloves, finely chopped
12 fresh sage leaves, chopped
2 large ripe tomatoes, peeled, seeded and coarsely chopped
120g/4oz Italian fontina or raclette, diced
6 tbsp freshly grated Parmesan

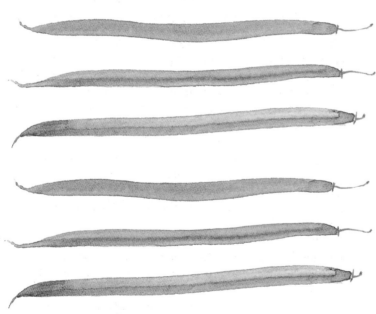

MINESTRA DI RISO, MANDORLE E PREZZEMOLO

RICE, ALMOND AND PARSLEY SOUP

Serves 4

120g/4oz almonds
1.25l/2pt chicken stock
1 chicken breast
120g/4oz Italian rice, preferably
Vialone Nano
3 tbsp chopped fresh flat-leaf
parsley
salt and freshly ground
black pepper

No clear soup like this can be successful without the basis of a good home-made stock. For this recipe I suggest a chicken stock instead of the more usual meat stock.

This is a delicate soup to be given to people who appreciate the balance of good ingredients.

1 Heat the oven to 220°C/425°F/Gas Mark 7.
2 Blanch the almonds in boiling water for 30 seconds. Drain and peel them. Place the almonds on a baking tray and bake for 10 minutes or until the aroma rises and the almonds are quite brown. Chop them to the size of grains of rice.
3 Heat the stock until boiling. Put in the chicken breast and cook gently for 10 minutes. Lift the breast out of the stock and place on a board.
4 Skin and bone the chicken breast. Cut the meat into small strips.
5 Slide the rice into the simmering stock. Simmer for 10 minutes, then stir in the strips of chicken, the parsley and almonds. Cook gently until the rice is *al dente*. Taste and add salt and pepper if necessary, then serve.

MINESTRONE

VEGETABLE SOUP WITH RICE

This is the classic minestrone with rice, or Minestrone alla Milanese, where rice is the starchy nourishment added to a vegetable soup.

1 Heat the oil and butter in a stockpot or a large saucepan, add the pancetta and sauté for 2 minutes. Add the onions, sage and parsley and fry gently for 5 minutes or so.

2 Mix in the garlic, carrots, celery and potatoes and fry for 2 minutes. Add the green beans and courgettes and sauté for a further couple of minutes.

3 Cover with 2.5l/4pt of hot water and add the tomatoes and salt and pepper to taste. Cover the pan and cook at a very low simmer for a minimum of $1\frac{1}{2}$ hours. Minestrone can be cooked for as long as 3 hours and it will be even better. Do not think that the vegetables will break; they do not.

4 About 30 minutes before you want to eat, add the cabbage and cook for 15 minutes. Then add the rice and the canned beans and stir well. Continue cooking uncovered at a steady simmer until the rice is *al dente*. Serve with a bowl of Parmesan on the side.

Minestrone is even better made a day in advance and warmed up. In the summer it is delicious cold, though not straight from the refrigerator.

Serves 6

2 tbsp olive oil
30g/1oz butter
120g/4oz unsmoked pancetta, or unsmoked streaky bacon, chopped
2 onions, coarsely chopped
4 or 5 fresh sage leaves, snipped
1 tbsp chopped fresh flat-leaf parsley
2 garlic cloves, chopped
2 carrots, diced
2 celery sticks, diced
2 potatoes, about 225g/½lb, diced
120/4oz green beans, cut into 2cm/¾in pieces
225g/½lb courgettes, diced
225g/½lb Italian canned plum tomatoes with their juice
salt and freshly ground black pepper
225g/½lb Savoy cabbage, cut into strips
150g/5oz Italian rice, preferably Semifino Padano or Vialone Nano
400g/14oz canned borlotti beans, drained
freshly grated Parmesan, to serve

RIPIENI E INSALATE DI RISO

RICE STUFFINGS AND SALADS

Two recipes for rice stuffings hardly do justice to an array of dishes in which rice is the primary ingredient of the stuffing. But I have chosen my favourites. While rice is commonly used as a stuffing for vegetables, its use in stuffing fish is less usual. The recipe for squid stuffed with rice is very interesting and very good; in fact, it is my preferred way of stuffing squid.

The versatility of rice is boundless. It even makes excellent salads, which is more than can be said for pasta.

I have also included in this section two of my favourite recipes for rice salads.

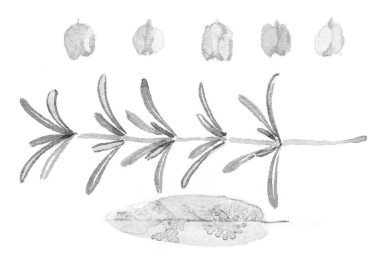

POMODORI RIPIENI DI RISO

—— TOMATOES STUFFED WITH BASIL-FLAVOURED RICE ——

Serves 4 as a first course

450g/1lb ripe tomatoes, all the
same size
salt and freshly ground
black pepper
90g/3oz Italian rice, preferably
Vialone Nano
2 garlic cloves, finely sliced
12 fresh basil leaves, snipped
1 egg
100ml/3½fl oz extra virgin
olive oil

The rice in this recipe is not previously cooked, but only soaked in oil so that it retains a stronger flavour. By the end of the cooking the tomatoes are very soft and become amalgamated with the rice, rather than being separate containers.

1 Wash and dry the tomatoes. Cut them across in half. Scoop out some of the seeds and discard. Scoop out all the pulp and the juice with a pointed spoon, taking care not to break the skin. Chop the pulp and put it in a bowl with the juice.

2 Sprinkle the insides of the tomato halves with salt and chill them.

3 Add the rice to the bowl together with the garlic and basil.

4 Beat the egg very lightly and mix thoroughly into the rice mixture. Add the oil, plenty of pepper and salt to taste. Mix again very well and leave for at least 3 hours.

5 Heat the oven to 190°C/375°F/Gas Mark 5.

6 Oil a large oven dish and place the tomato halves in it, cut side up. Fill them with the rice mixture, to come level with the tops of the tomatoes. Cover the dish with foil and bake until the rice is cooked, about 45 minutes. Serve hot.

CALAMARI RIPIENI DI RISO

SQUID STUFFED WITH RICE

Rice, a staple of the north, is sometimes used in fish dishes in Puglia, the heel of the Italian boot. The fish used there for this dish is cuttlefish. Although this is a fairly common species off the south coast of England, most of the best catch there is shipped straight to France and Spain. For this reason I prefer to use squid, which are easily available. Whenever I can I buy the local squid, large specimens with a very good flavour, much better than the small calamari which come from Italy and Spain. These are often frozen or, what is worse, appear to be fresh although in fact they have previously been frozen.

1 Ask your fishmonger to clean the squid, or do it yourself by following these instructions. Hold the sac in one hand and pull off the tentacles with the other hand. The contents of the sac will come out too. Cut the tentacles above the eyes. Squeeze out the thin bony beak in the centre of the tentacles. Peel off the skin from the sac and the flap. Remove the translucent backbone from inside the sac and rinse the sac and tentacles under cold water. Keep the sacs whole.

2 Cut the tentacles into small pieces and then chop them coarsely until they are about the same size as the grains of rice.

3 Put 2 tbsp of the oil in a sauté pan. Add the rice, chopped tentacles, parsley, garlic, chilli and lemon zest and sauté briskly for a few minutes to *insaporire* – let the mixture take up all the flavours.

4 Finely chop the anchovy fillets and stir into the mixture. Cook at a lower temperature for a minute or so. Taste and add salt and pepper, if necessary.

5 Heat the oven to 180°C/350°F/Gas Mark 4.

Serves 3–4 as a main course

4 large squid, about 1kg/2¼lb
6 tbsp olive oil
4 level tbsp cooked Italian rice, preferably Vialone Nano
3 tbsp chopped fresh flat-leaf parsley
2 garlic cloves, chopped
½ dried chilli, chopped
grated zest of ½ unwaxed lemon
2 salted anchovies, boned and rinsed, or 4 canned anchovy fillets, drained
salt and freshly ground black pepper
120ml/4fl oz dry white wine

6 Fill each squid sac with the rice mixture. Do not pack the stuffing too tight or the sac will burst during the cooking. Stitch up the opening with a needle and thread and lay the squid in a single layer, close to each other, in an oven dish. (I use a metal tin, because metal transmits the heat better than ceramic.)

7 Pour the rest of the oil and the wine over the squid. Cover the oven dish tightly with a piece of foil and bake for about 1 hour, until the squid are tender when pricked with a fork.

8 When they are done, transfer the squid to a carving board and allow to cool for 10 minutes. Slice off a very thin strip from the sewn end to eliminate the thread. Cut each sac into thick slices of about 2.5cm/1in. If you possess one, use an electric carving knife which will make this slicing very easy. Otherwise see that your knife is very sharp. Gently transfer the slices to a serving dish.

9 Taste the cooking juices. If bland, boil briskly until reduced and full of flavour. Spoon over the squid. You can serve the dish hot, warm or even at room temperature, which I personally prefer.

INSALATA DI RISO CON MOZZARELLA ED ACCIUGHE

RICE SALAD WITH MOZZARELLA AND ANCHOVY FILLETS

I strongly recommend using buffalo mozzarella for this dish. If possible, dress the rice 2 hours before serving.

1 Cook the rice in plenty of boiling salted water until just *al dente*. (Remember that when served cold, rice is better if a touch undercooked.) Drain the rice, rinse under cold water and drain again. Transfer the rice to a bowl and pat dry with kitchen paper towels. Add 2 tbsp of the oil and set aside to cool.

2 Chop the eggs and add to the rice, together with the mozzarella.

3 Chop the anchovy fillets and place in another bowl. Mix in the parsley, garlic and chilli. Beat in the remaining oil with a fork until the sauce thickens. Season with salt and pepper to taste.

4 Spoon this dressing into the rice and mix very thoroughly with two forks so as to separate all the grains. Taste and adjust the seasoning to your liking. Scatter the olives and capers here and there and serve cold, but not chilled.

Serves 4 as a first course

250g/9oz Italian rice, preferably Vialone Nano
salt and freshly ground black pepper
6 tbsp extra virgin olive oil
2 hard-boiled eggs
150g/5oz buffalo mozzarella, cut into small cubes
6 salted anchovies, boned and rinsed, or 12 canned anchovy fillets, drained
4 tbsp chopped fresh flat-leaf parsley
1 small garlic clove, very finely chopped
1 small dried chilli, seeded and crumbled
12 black olives
1 tbsp capers, rinsed and dried

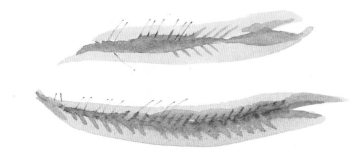

RISO E CECI IN INSALATA

RICE AND CHICK PEA SALAD

Serves 4

150g/5oz dried chick peas
salt and freshly ground
black pepper
1 tsp bicarbonate of soda
1 tbsp flour
1 small onion
1 celery stick
2 sprigs of fresh rosemary
4 fresh sage leaves
a few parsley stalks
2 garlic cloves
7 tbsp extra virgin olive oil
200g/7oz Italian rice,
preferably Vialone Nano or
Semifino Padano
1 garlic clove, finely chopped
a lovely bunch of fresh flat-leaf
parsley, finely chopped
225g/½lb best ripe tomatoes,
peeled and seeded
12 fresh basil leaves, snipped

It is surprising how two ingredients as modest as rice and chick peas can produce, when mixed together, such a really good and attractive dish.

Cook the chick peas properly until they are soft. In common with my compatriots, I find nothing more unpleasant than under-cooked pulses, as they are sometimes served in 'Britalian' restaurants. The rice should be *al dente*, not because of the over-praised 'contrast of texture', but simply because rice is good *al dente*. Chick peas, however, are good when soft.

1 Put the chick peas in a large bowl and cover with plenty of cold water. Mix the salt, bicarbonate of soda and flour with a little cold water to make a paste and stir this into the soaking water. This helps to tenderise the skin as well as the chick peas themselves. Leave to soak for at least 18 hours; 24 is better.

2 Rinse the chick peas and put them in a pot. (An earthenware stockpot is the best for cooking pulses because of earthenware's heat-retaining properties.) Add the onion and celery and cover with water to come about 8cm/3in over the chick peas. Place the pot on the heat.

3 Tie the rosemary, sage, parsley stalks and whole garlic cloves in a small piece of muslin to make a bundle and add to the pot. Bring to the boil, then lower the heat and cook, covered, until the chick peas are ready. The liquid should simmer rather than boil. Chick peas take 2–3 hours to cook. Add salt only when they are nearly done, as the salt tends to make the skin crack and wrinkle.

4 Drain the chick peas (you can keep the liquid for a bean or vegetable soup). Fish out and discard the onion, celery and herb bag. Transfer the chick peas to a bowl and toss, while still hot, with 2 tbsp of the oil.

5 Cook the rice in plenty of boiling salted water. Drain when just *al dente*. Mix into the chick peas.

6 Put the rest of the oil, the chopped garlic and chopped parsley in a small frying pan. Sauté for 2 minutes, stirring constantly.

7 Dice the tomatoes and mix into the *soffritto* – frying mixture. Cook for 1 minute and then spoon over the rice and chick pea mixture. Add the snipped fresh basil and plenty of pepper. Toss thoroughly but lightly. Taste and check the salt. Serve at room temperature.

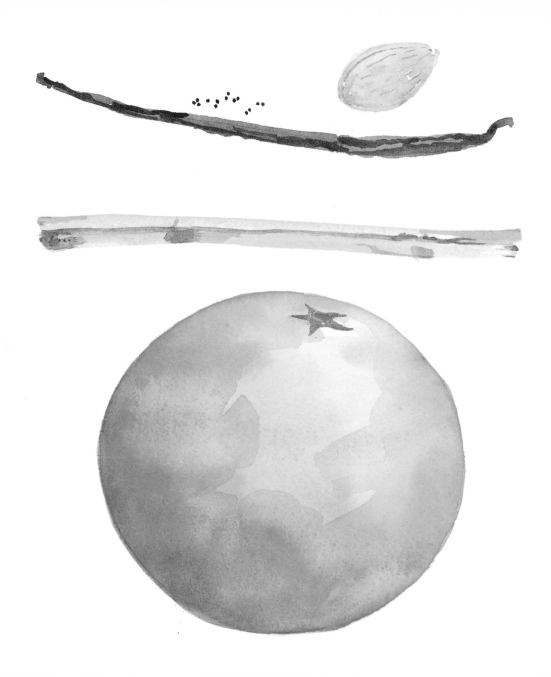

RISI DOLCI

SWEET RICE DISHES

This little book of homage to my home town's staple food ends with three recipes for sweets, although, ironically, they do not come from Milan. The rice cake and rice fritters are from Tuscany and the Black Rice is, oddly enough, from Sicily.

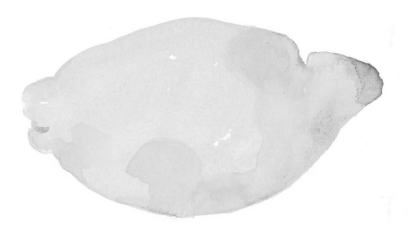

TORTA DI RISO

RICE CAKE WITH ALMONDS AND SULTANAS

Serves 8

750ml/1¼pt full-fat milk
180g/6oz caster sugar
a strip of unwaxed lemon zest, yellow part only
a piece of vanilla pod, 2.5cm/1in long
a piece of cinnamon stick, 5cm/2in long
salt
150g/5oz Italian rice, preferably Arborio
4 tbsp sultanas
2 tbsp dark rum
100g/3½oz almonds, blanched and peeled (see page 40)
4 eggs, separated
grated zest of ½ unwaxed lemon
butter and dried breadcrumbs for the tin
icing sugar, to finish

This is the Florentine version of a cake that is popular all over central Italy. I like to make it with Arborio rice, as it swells during the cooking while absorbing the milk. You can add other ingredients according to your taste, for instance chocolate pieces and/or candied peel. What you will have is a firm yet moist cake, not a pudding, that is equally delicious with a dollop or two of thick cream on top or without cream. The cake should not be served until at least the day after making it, to allow the flavours to blend.

1 Put the milk, 30g/1oz of the sugar, the strip of lemon zest, vanilla pod, cinnamon stick and a pinch of salt in a saucepan and bring to the boil. Add the rice and stir well with a wooden spoon. Cook, uncovered, over very low heat for about 35 minutes, stirring frequently, until the rice has absorbed the milk and is soft. Set aside to cool.

2 Heat the oven to 180°C/350°F/Gas Mark 4.

3 Put the sultanas in a bowl and pour over the rum. Leave them to puff up.

4 Spread the almonds on a baking tray and toast them in the oven for about 10 minutes or until they are quite brown. Shake the tray occasionally to prevent them from burning. Cool them a little, then chop them coarsely.

5 Remove the strip of lemon zest, the vanilla pod and cinnamon stick from the rice and spoon the rice into a mixing bowl. (Wash and dry the vanilla pod so that you can use it again.) Incorporate 1 egg yolk at a time into the rice, mixing well after each addition. Add the remaining sugar, the almonds, sultanas with the rum

and the grated lemon zest to the rice and egg mixture and mix everything together thoroughly.

6 Whisk the egg whites until they are stiff, then fold them gently into the rice mixture.

7 Butter a 20cm/8in spring-clip tin. Line the bottom with grease-proof paper and butter the paper. Sprinkle all over with bread-crumbs to coat evenly and shake out excess crumbs.

8 Spoon the rice mixture into the prepared tin. Bake in the oven (still at the same temperature) for about 45 minutes or until a thin skewer or a wooden cocktail stick inserted in the middle of the cake comes out just moist. The cake should also have shrunk from the side of the tin.

9 Leave the cake to cool in the tin, then remove the clipped band and turn the cake over onto a plate. Remove the base of the tin and the lining paper. Place a round serving platter on the cake and turn it over again. Leave for at least 24 hours before serving the cake. Sprinkle with icing sugar before serving.

RISO NERO

BLACK RICE PUDDING

Serves 6

600ml/1pt full-fat milk
75g/2½oz Italian rice, preferably
Vialone Nano
90g/3oz sugar
100g/3½oz almonds, blanched,
peeled and chopped
pinch of salt
pinch of ground cinnamon
150ml/¼pt black coffee
45g/1½oz bitter chocolate,
flaked or grated
grated zest of 1 small orange
15g/½oz unsalted butter
150ml/¼pt whipping cream

There are not many rice dishes in Sicily, but this is one of the few Sicilian contributions to the vast range of Italian rice sweets. It is different from the rice desserts of the central Italian regions – the motherland of rice cakes and puddings – because it contains a high proportion of chocolate and coffee.

In Sicily this dish is served without cream, but even though I am not a cream fan, I must admit that cream lightens the almondy-chocolate flavour of the riso nero.

---

1 Put the milk, rice, sugar, almonds, salt, cinnamon and coffee in a heavy-bottomed saucepan. Bring to the boil and simmer until the rice is very soft, about 1 hour, stirring frequently. If you use a flame diffuser you can leave it a little longer, but be careful because the milky rice tends to stick to the bottom of the pan.

2 Draw the pan off the heat and mix in the chocolate and the orange zest.

3 Grease a 900ml/1½pt pudding basin with the butter. Spoon in the rice mixture and leave to cool. When cold, cover with cling film and put in the fridge to chill.

4 Free the pudding all round with a palette knife and turn it out onto a round platter.

5 Whip the cream and spread it all over the brown dome just before serving.

ANTICA E RINOMATA RISERIA

FERRON

(La famosa "Pila Vecchia")
FONDATA NEL 1650

ISOLA DELLA SCALA
VERONA

IL RISO CHE FA BUONI SAN GUE

RISO SEMIFINO
VIALONE NANO
RICE FOR RISOTTO

Product of Italy
PESO NETTO 1000 g ℮
NET WEIGHT: 85 2 oz (2.2 lbs)

FRITTELLE DI RISO

RICE FRITTERS

Serves 4

600ml/1pt full fat milk
pinch of salt
75g/2½oz Italian rice,
preferably Semifino Padano or
Vialone Nano
2 tbsp sugar
pared zest of ½ unwaxed orange,
in strips
pared zest of ½ unwaxed lemon,
in strips
2 size 2 eggs
vegetable oil for frying
icing sugar, to decorate

These fritters are sold and eaten in the streets of Florence as a *merenda*, or snack.

1 Put the milk, salt, rice, sugar and fruit zest in a heavy-bottomed saucepan. Bring slowly to the boil, stirring frequently. Cook, uncovered, at a very low heat for about 1 hour or until the rice has absorbed all the milk and is very soft. Stir frequently. Spoon the mixture into a bowl and allow to cool a little.

2 Lightly beat the eggs to break the white, then incorporate into the rice mixture. Mix very well and place the bowl in the fridge. If possible chill for 1 hour so the mixture firms, which will make it easier to shape and fry.

3 Heat the oil to 170°C/325°F in a wok or a frying pan. At this temperature a piece of stale bread should brown in 50 seconds.

4 Discard the orange and lemon zest from the rice mixture. With a metal spoon pick up some of the rice mixture – a dollop about the size of a large walnut – and with the help of a second spoon slide it into the oil. Fry the fritters in batches until they are golden on both sides. Retrieve them with a fish slice and place on kitchen paper towels to drain.

5 Sprinkle each fritter very generously with sifted icing sugar before serving. They are good hot or cold.

I DOLCI

'Il vero lusso di una mensa sta nel dessert'
The real luxury of a meal lies in the dessert.
From *Il Piacere* by Gabriele D'Annunzio

DOLCI

Italians love sweets, although they only eat them on special occasions. An everyday meal ends with fresh fruit; sweets are kept for Sundays, parties, family gatherings, religious days and village *feste*.

Dolci developed differently in northern, central and southern Italy. The dolci of the north are often little more than sweet breads, the panettone milanese being the prime example. The dolci of central Italy are richer, with lots of spices, nuts, candied peel and honey, as in the panforte from Siena or the *certosino* from Bologna. It was also in this part of the country that there originated the '*dolci al cucchiaio*' (sweets that can be eaten with a spoon such as the *zuppe inglesi*, or trifles) of Emilia-Romagna and Tuscany. In southern Italy the protagonists of dolci are almonds and candied fruits, a heritage from Arab cooking. And it is here that dolci reach the highest level of culinary art.

This being Italy, there are, of course, many exceptions to this rule. After all, the birthplace of zabaglione – the *dolce al cucchiaio* par excellence – is Piedmont in the north, while a *ciambella* – sweet ring-shaped bread made with potatoes, eggs and flour – is a traditional dolce of Apulia.

As they are eaten on feast days, dolci are even more regional than other kinds of food. Every patron saint, every feast day of the year, has its own special dolce, in every town in Italy. The region that has more special occasions, and more legends, associated with its dolci is Sicily. There are biscuits called *frutti di morte* – fruits of death – made with *pasta reale* – almond paste – that are eaten at the end of a meal on All Soul's day, 2 November. The *sfinci di San Giuseppe* are a sort of fritter eaten on St Joseph's day, 19 March. For Easter Sunday a magnificent *agnello pasquale* – Easter lamb – is made in Sicily with a pastry, strongly flavoured with cloves, that is moulded in the shape of a lamb.

Some of these special dolci have become so popular that they are now eaten all year round, not only in Italy but abroad, as is the case with panettone and panforte, both originally eaten only at Christmas. Others are still very localised and known only in the place where they are made. When I was in Sicily recently I ate some superb soft biscuits called *olivette di Sant'Agata*. They were made of marzipan, sugar, rum and vanilla, and are a speciality of Catania, made originally on the saint's day of Sant'Agata, a local martyr. I had never heard of *olivette* before, yet they are the best almond-based sweets I have ever had. Our Sicilian hostess insisted that we drive many, many miles along the motorway to an old fashioned *pasticceria* in Catania to buy 'the only *olivette* worth eating'. The lengths Italians will go in their search for excellence, as far as food is concerned, never ceases to amaze me.

The tradition of excellence in Italian dolci goes back a long way. Writing in Naples at the beginning of the nineteenth century, Lady Blessington, a friend of Emma Hamilton, commented, 'Italian confectionery and ices are far superior to those of the French and the English, and their variety is infinite.' A passage from *Il Gattopardo* by Giuseppe Tomasi di Lampedusa gives a good idea of what Lady Blessington meant. He describes how, at the great ball, the table was covered with pink parfaits, champagne parfaits, grey parfaits which parted creaking under the blade of the cake knife; a violin melody in major of candied morello cherries; acid notes of yellow pineapples; and the *trionfi della gola* – triumphs of gluttony – with the opaque green of their pistachio paste, and the shameless *minni di virgini* – virgins' breasts.'

Note: all spoon measures should be level.

TORTE E CROSTATE

CAKES AND TARTS

The emphasis of this section is on cakes containing fruit and nuts.

In Italy, cakes, even the drier sort, are often eaten as part of a meal. Cakes are also served mid-morning or after supper, when they are traditionally accompanied by a glass of wine. Wine, after all, used to be the cheapest beverage, one that even poor people in the country could afford. They made their own wine, while tea or coffee had to be bought.

The section ends with two recipes for tarts. Tarts are not as common in Italy as in France, but the ones I have chosen are very characteristic and, so far as I know, are only to be found in their place of origin.

In all the cake and biscuit recipes, I recommend the use of Italian 00 flour. This is a high-quality flour with very little flavour and very good raising properties. It is available from specialist Italian shops.

TORTA DI CIOCCOLATO FARCITA DI ZABAIONE

CHOCOLATE AND ZABAGLIONE CAKE

Serves 8

60g/2oz bitter chocolate
100g/3½oz unsalted butter, at room temperature
180g/6oz caster sugar
3 size-2 eggs, at room temperature, separated
1½ tbsp dark rum
100g/3½oz plain flour, preferably Italian 00 (see page 7)
100g/3½oz potato flour
1½ tsp baking powder
½ tsp salt
1 tsp lemon juice
unsalted butter and flour for the tin
150ml/¼pt double cream

For the zabaglione

4 size-2 egg yolks
5 tbsp caster sugar
a piece of vanilla pod
120ml/4 fl oz dry Marsala or medium sherry

My editor, Gillian Young, sampled this cake when she came to tea the other day, and declared it very well worth writing about. This endorsed my opinion, because it has the perfect balance of chocolate, sugar and alcohol. The zabaglione, poured on each half of the cake, partly sinks into the sponge. This makes a thin layer in the middle of the cake, giving it two slightly different textures.

Like many Italian cooks, I often replace half the plain flour with the same amount of potato flour for more lightness in the sponge; it is these quantities which are given below.

1 Heat the oven to 130°C/250°F/Gas Mark ½. Break the chocolate into small pieces, put in a heatproof bowl and warm in the oven until the chocolate has melted. Set the chocolate aside. Turn the oven heat up to 190°C/375°F/Gas Mark 5.

2 Beat the butter until it is soft. Add the sugar and beat together until pale and creamy. Gradually beat in the egg yolks, rum and melted chocolate.

3 Sift the two flours, baking powder and salt through a fine sieve twice.

4 Whisk the egg whites with the lemon juice until stiff but not dry. (The lemon juice, being acid, helps to stabilise the froth without increasing its volume.)

5 Add 1 tbsp of the flour mixture and 1 tbsp of the egg white and fold into the chocolate mixture with a high movement, using a metal spoon. Continue adding alternate spoonfuls of flour mixture and egg white.

6 Generously butter a 20cm/8in spring-clip cake tin. Sprinkle with flour, then shake out excess flour. Spoon the cake mixture into the tin and place in the oven. The cake will be cooked in about 45 minutes. To see if it is ready, insert a wooden cocktail stick into the middle; it should come out dry.

7 Leave the cake in the tin for about 10 minutes to settle and then turn it out on to a wire rack to cool.

8 Meanwhile, make the zabaglione. Put the egg yolks, sugar and vanilla in a round-bottomed metal bowl or in the upper part of a double boiler. Beat well with a small balloon whisk. Beat in the Marsala. Set the bowl in a bain-marie, i.e. in a pan containing simmering water, or set the double boiler pan over the bottom pan. Continue beating until the mixture is dense and thick.

9 Cut the cake horizontally in half. Make some slits in the cut face of each half and pour about two-thirds of the zabaglione all over them. Do this slowly to allow the zabaglione to penetrate into the sponge. Put the two halves together again. Refrigerate for at least 6 hours.

10 Whip the cream until stiff. Whisk the rest of the zabaglione until it is thick again, then mix evenly with the cream. Cover the top of the cake with this mixture. Keep the cake in the fridge until you want to serve it.

TORTA DI CIOCCOLATO CON LE PERE

CHOCOLATE AND PEAR CAKE

Serves 4–6

75g/2½oz bitter chocolate, broken into small pieces
75g/2½oz unsalted butter, at room temperature
75g/2½oz icing sugar, sifted
1 egg, at room temperature, separated
2 egg yolks, at room temperature
pinch of ground cinnamon
pinch of salt
120g/4oz plain flour, preferably Italian 00 (see page 7)
1 large, ripe but firm William's pear, about 225g/½lb
unsalted butter and flour for the tin
icing sugar, to decorate

I make this cake in a loaf tin, as it used to be made at home for our *merenda* – afternoon tea. If you want to serve it as a dessert, I suggest making it in a 15cm/6in round tin.

1 Heat the oven to 130°C/250°F/Gas Mark ½. Put the chocolate in a heatproof bowl and melt it in the oven. Remove from the oven and keep in a warm place. Turn the oven heat up to 180°C/350°F/Gas Mark 4.

2 Beat the butter until really soft. I use a hand-held electric mixer. Gradually add the icing sugar while beating constantly, then beat until light and pale yellow. (If you add all the sugar at once and start beating butter and sugar together, you will find the sugar flying everywhere except in the butter.) Add the 3 egg yolks, cinnamon, salt and melted chocolate.

3 Whisk the egg white until stiff but not dry and then fold it into the mixture by the spoonful, alternating it with spoonfuls of flour. Fold lightly but thoroughly.

4 Peel and core the pear and cut it into 1cm/½in cubes. Mix lightly into the mixture.

5 Butter a loaf tin that is approximately 17.5 × 10 × 5cm/7 × 4 × 2in. Sprinkle in 1 tbsp of flour, shake the tin so the flour covers all the surface and then throw away the excess flour. Spoon the cake mixture into the tin. Bake for about 50 minutes or until the sides of the cake have shrunk from the tin and the cake is dry in the middle – test by inserting a wooden cocktail stick.

6 Remove the tin from the oven, unmould the cake on to a wire rack and leave to cool.

7 Sprinkle with sifted icing sugar just before serving.

TORTA DI NOCI

WALNUT CAKE

Serves 6–8

120g/4oz unsalted butter, at room temperature
180g/6oz icing sugar, sifted
3 size-2 eggs, at room temperature, separated
150g/5oz walnut pieces
120g/4oz plain flour, preferably Italian 00 (see page 7)
$\frac{1}{2}$ tbsp baking powder
pinch of salt
grated zest of 1 unwaxed lemon
$\frac{1}{4}$ tsp lemon juice
unsalted butter and dried breadcrumbs for the tin
icing sugar, to decorate

Buy your walnuts from a shop with a quick turnover so that they will not be old and rancid. Better still, buy the nuts in their shells at Christmas time and shell them yourself. Keep them in the freezer.

1 Heat the oven to 180°C/350°F/Gas Mark 4.

2 Beat the butter until very soft. Gradually beat in the icing sugar to make a smooth thick cream. Use a hand-held electric mixer, if you have one.

3 Lightly beat the egg yolks together with a fork, then add gradually to the butter cream, mixing thoroughly to incorporate.

4 Put the walnuts in a food processor and process until very coarsely ground while pulsing the machine. The nuts should be grainy, not ground fine. Stir into the butter mixture.

5 Sift the flour, baking powder and salt together and fold into the butter mixture with the lemon zest.

6 Whisk the egg whites with the lemon juice until stiff but not dry and fold into the mixture, using a metal spoon and lifting it high to incorporate more air.

7 Generously butter a 20cm/8in spring-clip cake tin. Sprinkle with breadcrumbs, shake the tin to cover all the surface and then shake out excess crumbs. Spoon the cake mixture into the prepared tin.

8 Bake in the preheated oven for about 45 minutes or until the cake is done. Test by inserting a wooden cocktail stick into the middle of the cake; it should come out dry. Unclip the side band and turn the cake over on to a wire rack to cool.

9 Sprinkle lavishly with sifted icing sugar before serving.

TORTA DI RICOTTA

RICOTTA CAKE

I do believe that some of the best recipes come from family *ricettari* – recipe collections. These are recipes for dishes that are suited to home cooking, and have been tested and improved over the years by generations of cooks. This is such a one.

1 Soak the sultanas in hot water for 15 minutes to puff them up.
2 Reserve 1 tbsp of the caster sugar. Beat the butter with the remaining caster sugar until pale and creamy and then add the eggs, one at a time. When all the eggs have been incorporated, mix in the lemon zest, potato flour, baking powder and salt.
3 Heat the oven to 180°C/350°F/Gas Mark 4.
4 Press the ricotta through the small-hole disc of a food mill, or through a sieve, directly on to the other ingredients. Do not use a food processor as this would not aerate the ricotta. Fold the ricotta thoroughly into the mixture. Drain the sultanas, pat them dry with kitchen paper towels and fold into the mixture.
5 Generously butter a 25cm/10in spring-clip cake tin and sprinkle with the reserved caster sugar to coat the bottom and sides.
6 Spoon the ricotta mixture into the tin and bake for $1-1\frac{1}{4}$ hours or until the cake is done (it will shrink slightly from the sides of the tin). Leave to cool in the tin. Unmould the cake when cold and place on a flat serving dish. Sprinkle with plenty of sifted icing sugar just before serving.

Serves 10–12

120g/4oz sultanas
300g/10oz caster sugar
120g/4oz unsalted butter, at room temperature
4 size-2 eggs, at room temperature
grated zest of 1 unwaxed lemon
6 tbsp potato flour
1 tbsp baking powder
$\frac{1}{2}$ tsp salt
1kg/2$\frac{1}{4}$lb fresh ricotta
unsalted butter for the tin
icing sugar, to decorate

LA TORTA SBRISOLONA

CRUMBLY CAKE

Serves 6

120g/4oz almonds
120g/4oz granulated sugar
150g/5oz plain flour
120g/4oz coarse cornmeal
grated zest of 1 unwaxed lemon
pinch of salt
2 egg yolks
120g/4oz unsalted butter, at
room temperature
unsalted butter for the tin
icing sugar, to decorate

The word *sbrisolona* is derived from *briciola* (stress on the first syllable), meaning 'crumb', which is what this cake seems to consist of. If you want it less crumbly, you can cut it into slices with a sharp knife when it is still hot. But I find that part of its appeal is its rustic appearance, as well, of course, as its deliciousness. My husband's comment on it, as he munched, was, 'This cake is not just moreish; once you start eating it, you can't stop.'

It is an ideal cake to take with tea or coffee in the afternoon, or with sweet wine at any time of day.

1 Heat the oven to 200°C/400°F/Gas Mark 6.

2 Drop the almonds into a pan of boiling water and boil for 30 seconds after the water has come back to the boil. Drain and remove the skin by squeezing the almonds between your fingers. Spread them on a baking tray and toast them in the oven for 7 minutes or until golden brown. Turn the heat down to 180°C/350°F/Gas Mark 4.

3 Put the almonds in a food processor with 2 tbsp of the granulated sugar and process until they are reduced to a coarse powder.

4 In a bowl, mix the flour, cornmeal, the remaining granulated sugar, lemon zest, ground almonds and salt. Add the egg yolks and work with your hands until the mixture is crumbly.

5 Add the butter to the crumbly mixture and work again to incorporate it thoroughly, until the dough sticks together in crumbly mass.

6 Generously butter a 20cm/8in shallow round cake tin and line the bottom with siliconised baking parchment. Spread the mixture evenly in the tin, pressing it down with your hands. Bake for 40–45 minutes or until the cake is golden brown and a skewer inserted in the centre comes out dry.

7 Turn out the cake on to a wire rack and peel off the baking parchment. Leave to cool. Before serving, sprinkle the cake with sifted icing sugar.

This cake keeps very well for several days.

PANFORTE

SPICY CAKE FROM SIENA

Serves 8–10

60g/2oz candied fruit
60/2oz preserved ginger
150g/5oz mixed candied orange, lemon and citron peel
60g/2oz ground hazelnuts
100g/3½oz whole hazelnuts
100g/3½oz almonds
60g/2oz walnut pieces
1 tsp ground cinnamon
large pinch of freshly grated nutmeg
large pinch of ground cloves
large pinch of freshly ground white pepper
large pinch of ground ginger
large pinch of ground coriander
4 tbsp plain flour
1 tbsp cocoa powder
4 tbsp granulated sugar
4 tbsp clear honey
oil and rice paper for the tin
1 tbsp icing sugar

Panforte is one of the most ancient dolci. A reference to 'a spicy and honeyed bread' brought back to Siena from the Middle East appears in Dante's *Inferno*. It is the traditional Christmas cake of Siena, but is now available all the year round.

There are two kinds of panforte, a white panforte and a black one. The white is the older version. The black was created when cocoa arrived from the New World and became the fashionable ingredient.

My recipe contains a little cocoa and makes a softer panforte than the commercial one. I have also substituted preserved ginger for candied pumpkin, which is not available in this country. The ginger is an excellent substitute, both for its flavour and by being in keeping with the early origins of panforte, when spices, just arrived from the Orient, were used very prodigally as a show of wealth.

1 Heat the oven to 180°C/350°F/Gas Mark 4.
2 Coarsely chop all the candied fruit and peel and place in a bowl. (This can be done in a food processor: cut the candied fruits and peel into pieces, put in the food processor and process for a short time, while shaking the machine backwards and forwards. Do not reduce to a paste.)
3 Spread the ground hazelnuts and the whole hazelnuts on two baking trays. Toast the ground hazelnuts in the oven for about 5 minutes and the whole hazelnuts for 10 minutes. Shake the trays gently from time to time. Add the ground hazelnuts to the candied fruits in the bowl.
4 Allow the whole hazelnuts to cool slightly and then rub them, a few at a time, in a coarse towel to remove the skin. Place the

nuts in a coarse sieve and shake to separate the skin from the nuts. Chop the nuts coarsely and add to the bowl.

5 Chop the almonds and walnuts coarsely and add to the bowl.

6 Put aside $\frac{1}{2}$ tsp of the cinnamon. Sift the rest of the cinnamon, all the other spices, the flour and cocoa powder directly into the bowl. Mix well.

7 Put the granulated sugar and honey into a small saucepan. Cook over low heat until the sugar has completely dissolved. Add to the bowl and mix very well with your hands.

8 Line the bottom of a 17.5cm/7in loose-based flan tin with rice paper and grease the sides of the tin with oil. Press the mixture evenly into the tin. Leave to stand at room temperature for 5 hours or longer if possible.

9 Preheat the oven to 170°C/325°F/Gas Mark 3.

10 Put the remaining cinnamon and the icing sugar in a sieve and sprinkle over the top of the cake. Bake for about 50 minutes.

11 Remove from the oven and leave to cool for 10 minutes, then remove the panforte from the tin and cool completely on a wire rack. When cold, wrap in foil and store.

Panforte will keep for at least 2–3 months.

PASTIERA NAPOLETANA

NEAPOLITAN TART

Serves 8–10

250g/9oz dried whole wheat, to
be soaked, or 400g/14oz
canned cooked wheat
600ml/1pt full fat milk
pinch of salt
grated zest of $\frac{1}{2}$ lemon and
$\frac{1}{2}$ orange
piece of vanilla pod, about
5cm/2in long, or a few drops of
vanilla essence
$\frac{1}{2}$ tsp ground cinnamon
300g/10oz fresh ricotta
4 eggs, at room temperature,
separated
2 egg yolks
225g/8oz caster sugar
2 tbsp orange flower water
120g/4oz candied peel, cut into
tiny pieces
unsalted butter for the tin
icing sugar, to decorate

For the pastry
300g/10oz plain flour,
preferably Italian 00 (see
page 7)
6 tbsp icing sugar
pinch of salt
grated zest of $\frac{1}{2}$ unwaxed lemon
150g/5oz unsalted butter, cut
into small pieces
3 size-2 egg yolks

At Easter time, bakers and *pasticceri* in Naples compete with each other to produce the best *pastiere*, the beloved tart of the Neapolitans, made with whole wheat and ricotta. You can now buy whole wheat in cans, called Gran Pastiera, in Italian shops. It is good, and saves the long labour of soaking the grain.

1 If you are using dried whole wheat, soak the grains in cold water for 48 hours. Rinse and drain them.

2 Put the soaked wheat in a saucepan with the milk, salt, lemon and orange zest, the vanilla pod and cinnamon and bring to the boil. Simmer over the lowest possible heat for 3–4 hours or until the grain is cooked and tender. Leave it to cool for at least 8 hours (24 hours is better) to allow the grain to swell. Remove and discard the vanilla pod.

3 If you are using canned wheat, just add the lemon and orange zest, vanilla essence and cinnamon.

4 Make the pastry dough: sift the flour, sugar and salt onto a work surface. Mix in the lemon zest, then rub in the butter. Add the egg yolks and knead together briefly to make a smooth and compact dough. (The dough can also be made in a food processor.) Wrap and chill for at least 2 hours.

5 To make the filling, beat the ricotta with the 6 egg yolks. Add the caster sugar, orange flower water, candied peel and grain mixture. Mix very thoroughly.

6 Whisk the 4 egg whites until stiff but not dry. Fold into the grain and ricotta mixture lightly but thoroughly.

7 Heat the oven to 180°C/350°F/Gas Mark 4. Butter a 25cm/10in spring-clip cake tin. Roll out about two-thirds of the pastry dough and press into the tin, making sure it is of the same thickness all over the bottom and up the sides. Spoon in the filling.

8 Roll out the remaining dough and cut into long strips. Place the strips over the filling to form a lattice top. Bake for 45–50 minutes or until the filling is set and the pastry is golden brown. Allow to cool and then turn out. Dust with sifted icing sugar before serving.

LA CROSTATA DI BIETOLE

SWISS CHARD AND CRÈME
PÂTISSIÈRE TART

Serves 6

450g/1lb Swiss chard
3 tbsp granulated sugar
5 cloves
2 tbsp sultanas
2 tbsp pine nuts
20g/¾oz bitter chocolate, cut
into small pieces
icing sugar, to decorate

For the pastry

225g/8oz plain flour, preferably
Italian 00 (see page 7)
60g/2oz caster sugar
2 pinches of salt
90g/3oz unsalted butter, cut
into small pieces
2 egg yolks
2 tbsp hot milk

For the crème pâtissière

300ml/½pt full-fat milk
pared strip of unwaxed
lemon zest
pared strip of unwaxed
orange zest
1 cinnamon stick
piece of vanilla pod
2 egg yolks
50g/1¾oz caster sugar
2 tbsp plain flour

I had this extraordinary tart at the San Martino restaurant in London. I find it extraordinary because of the use of Swiss chard in a sweet dish, something I had never met before. Yet the owner of the San Martino assured me that in his native province of Lucca the tart is called 'La Torta della Nonna' – grandmother's tart, a name that proves its popularity.

It is quite delicious, as well as being mysterious in its remote chocolatey taste.

1 To make the pastry dough, pile the flour on the work surface, mix in the sugar and salt and rub in the butter. Add the egg yolks and hot milk and work quickly to a smooth dough. Form a ball, wrap and chill for at least 2 hours.

2 Roll out two-thirds of the dough into a circle 5mm/¼in thick. Line a 17.5cm/7in loose-based flan tin with the circle of dough, pressing firmly into the corners. Put back into the fridge while you prepare the filling.

3 To make the crème pâtissière, put the milk in a saucepan, add all the flavourings and bring to the boil. Draw off the heat and leave to infuse for about 1 hour.

4 Put the egg yolks and sugar into a heavy-bottomed saucepan and beat until the eggs are pale yellow and creamy. Add the flour gradually.

5 Strain the milk and return to its pan. Bring back to simmering point. Off the heat, add very gradually to the egg and flour mixture, beating constantly.

6 Put the saucepan over low heat and bring to a simmer, while stirring constantly. Simmer for 5 minutes to cook the flour and

then draw off the heat. Place the base of the pan in a sink of cold water to cool quickly.

7 Remove the Swiss chard stalks from the leaves; reserve the stalks for another dish. Bring 300ml/½pt of water to the boil. Add the granulated sugar and cloves and stir to dissolve the sugar. Plunge in the Swiss chard leaves, stir well and cook until tender. Drain, but do not squeeze the liquid out. Set aside.

8 Heat the oven to 200°C/400°F/Gas Mark 6.

9 Spread a little of the crème pâtissière over the bottom of the pastry case. Cover with about half the Swiss chard and sprinkle with half the sultanas, pine nuts and chocolate pieces. Spread on another layer of crème, then more Swiss chard and finally the remaining crème. Sprinkle the remaining sultanas, pine nuts and chocolate pieces over the top.

10 Roll out the remaining pastry. Cut 6 strips, each about 1 cm/½in wide, and lay them on top of the tart in a criss-cross fashion to form a lattice. Bake for 20 minutes or until the pastry is golden brown. Allow to cool in the tin. When cold, turn out and sprinkle the top with sifted icing sugar.

BISCOTTI E FRITTELLE

BISCUITS AND FRITTERS

If you open a regional Italian cookery book, you will find more recipes for biscuits than for any other type of sweet. This is because, in Italy, sweets tend to be eaten at any time of day, whereas to have a pudding at the end of a meal is unusual. Biscuits are often eaten casually, as a snack, with a glass of wine, sitting round the kitchen table.

From the vast range of sweet fritters in Italy I have picked two recipes which I particularly like. Fritters are amongst the most ancient of foods; in Roman times they were prepared and eaten in the streets on pagan feast days, just as they are today at village feasts. Frying, after all, is the most immediate of cooking methods, and requires only a saucepan full of oil.

In all the cake and biscuit recipes, I recommend the use of Italian 00 flour. This is a high-quality flour with very little flavour and very good raising properties. it is available from specialist Italian shops.

BACI DI DAMA

LADY'S KISSES

Makes about 35 biscuits

120g/4oz best almonds
120g/4oz caster sugar
120g/4oz unsalted butter, at
room temperature
1 tsp pure vanilla essence
pinch of salt
120g/4oz plain flour, preferably
Italian 00 (see page 27)
unsalted butter for the trays
100g/3½oz bitter chocolate

The name of these biscuits is just as lovely as the biscuits themselves. They are a speciality of Tortona, a town in southern Piedmont.

1 Heat the oven to 180°C/350°F/Gas Mark 4.

2 Blanch the almonds in boiling water for 30 seconds. Drain and squeeze them in your fingers to remove the skins. Spread them on a baking tray and put in the oven for 5 minutes to dry thoroughly.

3 Put the almonds in a food processor. Add 1–2 tbsp of the sugar (this absorbs the oil from the nuts) and process to a fine powder. Add the butter, vanilla and salt and process again until the mixture is very creamy. Transfer to a bowl.

4 Sift the flour into the bowl. Fold in the flour very thoroughly to make a dough.

5 Break off pieces of the dough, the size of cherries, and roll them into balls between the palms of your hands. Place them on buttered baking trays, spacing them about 2cm/¾in apart. Bake for about 15 minutes or until golden brown. Leave to cool on the trays for about 5 minutes and then transfer to a wire rack to cool completely.

6 Melt the chocolate in a bain-marie. When the biscuits are cold, spread a little of the chocolate over one biscuit and make a sandwich by sticking another biscuit to the chocolate.

I BISCOTTI DELLA NONNA CATERINA
MY GRANDMOTHER'S BISCUITS

There is an infinite number of 'Torte della Nonna', but unfortunately none I can claim for <u>my</u> grandmother. However, she made these lovely biscuits that are ideal for serving with ice-creams or mousses, or to have with coffee.

Makes about 24 biscuits

2 size-2 egg yolks
2 tbsp rum
120g/4oz caster sugar
150g/5oz plain flour, preferably Italian 00 (see page 27)
pinch of salt
100g/3½oz unsalted butter, very soft but not melted
butter and flour for the trays

1 Heat the oven to 180°C/350°F/Gas Mark 4.

2 Beat the egg yolks with the rum. Add the sugar and beat hard until pale.

3 Sift the flour with the salt and add gradually to the egg and sugar mixture, stirring hard the whole time.

4 Add the butter and beat until the mixture is well blended.

5 Butter two baking trays. To form the biscuits, dampen your hands, pick up a little dollop of the biscuit dough and shape it into a round. Place the rounds on the trays, leaving about 5cm/2in between each one, because the mixture spreads out a lot while cooking. Bake for 15–20 minutes or until deep gold.

6 Remove the trays from the oven and transfer the biscuits to a wire rack to cool.

These biscuits will keep well for a week in an airtight tin.

LE BISSE

S-SHAPED BISCUITS

Makes about 40 biscuits

3 eggs
180g/6oz caster sugar
150ml/¼pt vegetable or olive oil
grated zest of 1 unwaxed lemon
500g/1lb 2oz plain flour,
preferably Italian 00 (see
page 27)
pinch of salt
oil for baking trays

A *bissa* is a water snake in Venetian dialect, which explains the name of these little biscuits. They are to be found in any bakery or *pasticceria* in Venice, but they can easily be made at home. Use an oil without flavour.

1 In a large bowl, whisk the eggs with the sugar until pale and frothy. Add the oil and lemon zest, then fold in the flour and salt. Knead well. Wrap the dough and chill it for about 1 hour.

2 Preheat the oven to 220°C/425°F/Gas Mark 7.

3 Grease 2 large baking trays with a little oil.

4 To shape each biscuit, take a little ball of dough and roll it into a sausage shape a little more than 1cm/½in thick and 12.5cm/5in long. Curve into the form of an 'S' and set on a baking tray.

5 Bake for 5 minutes, then reduce the heat to 180°C/350°F/Gas Mark 4 and bake for a further 10–15 minutes or until pale golden. Cool slightly on the baking trays before transferring to a wire rack to cool completely.

CROSTOLI TRENTINI

FRITTERS FROM NORTHERN ITALY

At Carnival time, every bakery or *pasticceria* in northern and central Italy makes a show of huge trays piled high with puffy golden fritters sprinkled with icing sugar. They are the traditional Carnival fare, made in different shapes in various regions. Thus there are *cenci*, meaning rags, in Tuscany, *chiacchiere*, chatterings, in Lombardy, *galani*, ribbons, in Venice and *sfrappole* in Emilia. The dough varies only a little. What changes is the shape.

The original crostoli from Trentino and Friuli are strips of dough tied together in a loose knot, but they are often cut, as in my recipe, which is easier and quicker. If you serve them at the end of a meal, hand round a bowl of whipped cream to dollop over the crostoli.

Serves 6

150g/5oz plain flour, preferably
Italian 00 (see page 27)
1½ tbsp caster sugar
½ tsp baking powder
pinch of salt
30g/1 oz unsalted butter, at
room temperature
1 size-2 egg yolk
3 tbsp grappa (Italian eau-de-vie)
or white rum
1–2 tbsp semi-skimmed milk
oil for frying
icing sugar, to decorate

1 Set aside 2 tbsp of flour. Put the rest of the flour on a work surface. Mix in the caster sugar, baking powder and salt. Make a well and put in the butter, egg yolk, grappa and milk. Mix everything together, kneading until the dough is well blended. If it is too hard add a little more milk; if too soft add some of the reserved flour. You can also make the dough in a food processor.

2 Knead the dough for at least 5 minutes as you would with bread or pasta dough. The dough should become smooth and elastic. Make a ball, wrap and leave at room temperature for 1 hour or longer.

3 Roll out the dough <u>very</u> thinly, using either a rolling pin or, better, a hand cranked pasta machine. If you are using the machine, roll through the last notch. The thinness of the dough is the secret of good crostoli.

4 Using a pastry wheel, cut the strips of dough into lasagne-size rectangles. Make 3 parallel slashes in the middle of each rectangle.

5 Heat enough frying oil to come two-thirds of the way up the sides of a frying pan or a wok. When the oil is very hot (a piece of stale bread should take 50 seconds to brown) fry the dough shapes in batches until pale gold and puffy. Lift the crostoli out of the oil with a fish slice and place on kitchen paper towels to drain.

6 Before serving, pile the crostoli on a dish, sprinkling every layer with sifted icing sugar. They are excellent hot or cold.

FRITTELLE DI SEMOLINO

SEMOLINA FRITTERS

These are other Carnival fritters from northern Italy. In my home they were always served with apple fritters and, of course, crostoli (see previous recipe).

Makes about 24 fritters

1l/1¾pt full fat milk
100g/3½oz granulated sugar
pared strip of unwaxed lemon zest
120g/4oz unsalted butter
pinch of salt
250g/9oz semolina
3 size-2 egg yolks
oil for frying
2 eggs
225g/8oz dried breadcrumbs
icing sugar, to decorate

1 Bring the milk slowly to the simmer with the granulated sugar, lemon zest, butter and salt, stirring frequently to dissolve the sugar.

2 Add the semolina in a slow stream while beating hard with a wooden spoon to prevent lumps forming. Continue stirring and cooking over low heat for 10 minutes. The mixture will be quite stiff. Draw off the heat and allow to cool for 15 minutes or so. Remove and discard the lemon zest.

3 Mix in the egg yolks, one at a time, beating well to incorporate after each addition.

4 Spread the semolina mixture on a board or flat dish to a thickness of about 2.5cm/1in. Level it down evenly with a damp spatula and leave it to cool completely. You can leave it overnight.

5 Cut the semolina into 2.5cm/1in wide strips and then cut the strips across to make lozenges.

6 Heat oil in a wok or in a deep frying pan to 175°C/330°F – hot enough for a cube of stale bread to brown in 50 seconds.

7 Meanwhile, lightly beat the 2 whole eggs in a bowl and spread the breadcrumbs in a dish. Dip a piece of semolina into the egg and then coat with breadcrumbs, patting them into the semolina.

8 Fry, in 2 or 3 batches, to a lovely gold colour and then put into a dish lined with kitchen paper towels to drain.

9 Serve hot or cold, lavishly sprinkled with sifted icing sugar.

DOLCI AL CUCCHIAIO

PUDDINGS

In this section I have collected eight recipes for dolci that are served at dinner parties, some famous, some little known, some elaborate and rich, others simple and modest, but all good and typically Italian.

TIRAMISU

MASCARPONE PUDDING

Serves 6

150ml/¼pt strong espresso
coffee
3tbsp brandy
60g/2oz bitter chocolate
2 eggs, at room temperature,
separated
1 egg yolk
4 tbsp caster sugar
250g/9oz mascarpone
about 20 Savoiardi biscuits

For the decoration
coffee beans
candied violets (optional)

A book on dolci would hardly be complete without including the most popular of them all, Tiramisù. Surprisingly, considering its popularity, Tiramisù is a relatively new arrival even on the Italian scene. Up to 20 years ago it was only known in the region where it originated, the Veneto.

Savoiardi are available from Italian delicatessens. If you cannot find them, make your own sponge finger biscuits – ordinary sponge fingers or boudoir biscuits from a supermarket will not be absorbent enough.

1 Mix together the coffee and brandy.

2 Grate about one-quarter of the chocolate and cut the rest into small pieces.

3 Beat the 3 egg yolks with the sugar until very pale and softly peaked. Fold the mascarpone in gradually and mix very thoroughly until the mixture is smooth and does not show any lumps.

4 Whisk the 2 egg whites until stiff but not dry and fold gradually into the mascarpone and egg yolk mixture.

5 Dip the biscuits, one at a time, into the coffee and brandy mixture, turning them over once or twice until they become pale brown. Lay 7 biscuits on the bottom of an oval dish, so as to make a base. Spread over one-quarter of the mascarpone cream and scatter with some chocolate pieces. Dip more biscuits into the coffee mixture and make another layer. Spread over one-quarter of the mascarpone cream and scatter with some chocolate pieces. Dip more biscuits into the coffee mixture and make another layer. Spread with another quarter of the cream and scatter with chocolate pieces. Cover with the last layer of moistened biscuits and spread with half the remaining cream.

6 Cover the pudding tightly and put it, with the reserved mascarpone cream, in the fridge to chill for about 6 hours.

7 Before serving, spread the reserved mascarpone cream over the top, smoothing it down neatly with a spatula. Sprinkle the grated chocolate all over the top and decorate with the coffee beans and with the optional candied violets.

CREMA MASCARPONE
MASCARPONE AND RUM CREAM

Similar to the ubiquitous Tiramisù, this dessert is lighter and more subtle. In my family it used to be called 'La Crema del Principe', and it is indeed a royal dessert, smooth and delicate.

The cream can be prepared ahead of time up to step 3. Add the egg whites no longer than 1 hour before serving. Serve with amaretti biscuits, whose dark, almondy flavour is ideal with this dessert.

Serves 4

2 size-2 eggs, separated
2 tbsp caster sugar
2 tbsp dark rum
225g/½lb mascarpone
1 tsp lemon juice
12 amaretti

1 Whisk the egg yolks with the sugar until light and mousse-like, then beat in the rum.

2 Press the mascarpone through a fine sieve and fold into the egg yolk mixture.

3 Whisk the egg whites with the lemon juice until stiff but not dry and fold gently into the mixture until the cream is smooth. Spoon the mixture into long stem glasses and place 1 amaretto on the top. Hand the rest of the amaretti round on a dish. Keep the cream chilled until ready to serve.

LA MERINGA FARCITA
MERINGUE FILLED WITH MARRONS GLACÉS,
CHOCOLATE AND CREAM

Serves 6–8

For the meringue
the whites of 4 size-2 eggs, at
room temperature
1 tsp lemon juice
225g/8 oz caster sugar

For the filling
the whites of 2 size-2 eggs
3 tbsp caster sugar
450ml/¾pt whipping cream
4 tbsp dark rum
225g/½lb marrons glacés, cut
into small pieces
100g/3½oz bitter chocolate, cut
into small pieces
2 tbsp pistachio nuts, blanched,
peeled and chopped
(see page 52)

The meringue in this recipe is Italian meringue, which is more reliable and less fragile than Swiss meringue made with uncooked whites of egg.

1 Heat the oven to 150°C/300°F/Gas Mark 2.

2 Make an Italian meringue as follows. Whisk the egg whites with the lemon juice until stiff. Put the bowl over a saucepan of simmering water and continue whisking while gradually adding the sugar. Whisk until the mixture is warm, silky looking and forming soft peaks.

3 Draw two 20cm/8in circles on siliconised baking parchment. Place the paper on 1 or 2 baking trays. Spoon the meringue over the two circles, smoothing it out with a palette knife. Place the trays in the oven and bake for about 45 minutes or until the meringue is set. Remove the meringue discs from the paper and allow to cool.

4 For the filling, whisk the egg whites in a bowl until stiff. Place the bowl over a saucepan of simmering water and gradually add the sugar, while whisking constantly. When the mixture is warm, remove from the heat and place the base of the bowl in a basin of cold water to cool. This stiff egg white mixture makes the filling lighter, both in texture and in substance.

5 Whip the cream. Fold in the egg white mixture.

6 Add the rum, marrons glacés, chocolate and pistachios and mix well until everything is evenly distributed.

7 Place one of the meringue discs on a flat dish. Spread two-thirds of the filling over it and put the other disc on top. Cover with the remaining filling. Chill for at least 6 hours before serving.

LE DITA DEGLI APOSTOLI

PANCAKES STUFFED WITH RICOTTA

The odd name of this recipe from Puglia, the heel of the Italian boot, means Apostles' Fingers. I can only suppose the pancakes were given this name because their appearance calls to mind long fingers, raised to give a blessing.

This is the recipe developed by my colleague and dear friend Alice Wooledge Salmon from the original recipe by the cookery teacher Paola Pettini, who showed us how to make the Dita during a recent stay in Puglia.

1 To make the pancakes, beat the eggs with the sugar. Mix in the flour and salt and then gradually add the milk while beating constantly. The batter should be fairly liquid. Leave to rest for 1 hour.

2 Meanwhile, prepare the stuffing. Sieve the ricotta into a bowl and fold in the cream and caster sugar. Add all the other ingredients and mix very thoroughly. Chill.

3 Make very thin pancakes in a 28cm/11in pan. (If not using a non-stick pan, grease it lightly with melted butter). You should get 12 large pancakes.

4 Lay the pancakes on the work surface and spread the stuffing thinly all over each one. Roll them up tightly

5 Cut each 'finger' into 3 or 4 pieces, place on a dish and sprinkle with sifted icing sugar. They are traditionally served cold.

Serves 8–10

For the pancakes
5 eggs
30g/1oz caster sugar
120g/4oz plain flour
pinch of salt
250ml/9 fl oz semi-skimmed milk
butter for frying pancakes

For the stuffing
600g/1¼lb fresh ricotta
3 tbsp double cream
250g/9oz caster sugar
grated zest of 1 unwaxed lemon
grated zest of 1 unwaxed orange
grated zest of 1 unwaxed clementine
1½ tbsp finely chopped candied peel
60g/2oz bitter chocolate, cut into small pieces
2 tbsp dark rum
icing sugar, to decorate

MELE ALLE MANDORLE E AL VINO BIANCO

SAUTÉED APPLES WITH ALMONDS
AND WHITE WINE

Serves 6

6 equal-sized large apples such
as Granny Smith or other sharp
dessert apples
1 unwaxed lemon, scrubbed and
washed
60g/2oz unsalted butter
3 cloves
150ml/$\frac{1}{4}$pt Calvados
60g/2oz caster sugar, or more
according to the sweetness of
the apples
120ml/4fl oz sweet white wine
$\frac{1}{2}$ tsp ground cinnamon
90g/3oz flaked almonds
300ml/$\frac{1}{2}$pt double cream
4 tbsp icing sugar, sifted

A lovely dessert, this combines the light, fresh flavour of fruit with the richness of a brandy-laced cream.

1 Peel the apples, then cut them in half and remove the cores. Make 6 incisions in the round side of each half, taking care not to cut right through it.

2 Remove the zest from half the lemon using a swivel-action potato peeler, taking care to leave behind the bitter white pith. Squeeze the juice.

3 Heat the butter in a very large sauté pan in which the apple halves will fit comfortably. Add the lemon zest and cloves to the butter and when the butter foam begins to subside, slide in the apples, cut side down. Sauté until golden, then turn the halves over and brown the round side. This will take about 8 minutes. Shake the pan occasionally to prevent the apples sticking.

4 Turn the heat up, pour over one-third of the Calvados and let it bubble away for 30 seconds. Turn the heat down to low and add the caster sugar, wine, lemon juice and 150ml/$\frac{1}{4}$pt of hot water. Cover the pan with the lid or a piece of foil and cook for 5 minutes. Turn the apples over carefully and continue cooking until they are tender. Cooking time varies according to the quality of the apples; do not overcook them or they may break. If necessary add a couple of spoonsful of hot water during the cooking.

5 When the apples are ready – test them by piercing them with the blade of a small knife through their thickest part – transfer them gently to a dish using a slotted spoon. Leave to cool.

6 Remove the lemon zest and cloves from the pan. Add the cinnamon and almonds and sauté over moderate heat for 5 minutes, stirring constantly, until the syrup is thick and the almonds are caramelized. Draw off the heat.

7 Whip the cream. Add the remaining Calvados and the icing sugar and whip again. Spread the cream over a shallow serving dish. Make 12 hollows in the cream with the back of a spoon and lay the apple halves in the hollows, cut side up. Spoon the syrup-coated almonds over the apples. Serve at room temperature.

FRUTTA COTTA AL FORNO
COMPÔTE OF MIXED FRUIT

The simplicity of this pudding should not deter you from trying it. The fruit, well cooked yet still in neat pieces, absorbs the flavour of the wine that, through the long cooking, has lost the taste of alcohol, which can be unpleasant when cooked with food. Buy prunes that don't need to be soaked.

1 Heat the oven to 180°C/350°F/Gas Mark 4.

2 Peel and core the pear and apples. Peel the banana and oranges. Slice them all quite thinly, keeping them separate.

3 Lay the sliced fruit in layers in a 1l/2pt oven dish, arranging it so that each fruit is topped with a different fruit. Scatter the prunes here and there and sprinkle with the lemon zest and sugar. Pour over the wine and cover the dish. Bake for 30 minutes.

4 Uncover the dish and press the fruit down with a slotted spoon to release more liquid. Bake for a further 15 minutes. Serve warm, with or without cream.

Serves 4

1 pear, Comice or William's
2 apples, Cox's or Granny Smith
1 banana
2 oranges
6 pitted prunes
grated zest of 1 small lemon
3 tbsp sugar
120ml/4fl oz robust red wine,
such as Barbera

ZUCCOTTO

FLORENTINE CREAM PUDDING

Serves 8–10

75g/2½oz almonds, blanched
and peeled (see page 28)
75g/2½oz hazelnuts
3 tbsp brandy
3 tbsp Amaretto
3 tbsp Maraschino or other
sweet liqueur
250g/9oz Madeira cake, cut
into 5mm/¼in thick slices
150g/5oz bitter chocolate
450ml/¾pt whipping cream
90g/3oz icing sugar, sifted

For the decoration
2 tbsp icing sugar
1 tbsp cocoa powder, sifted

A rich creamy pudding from Florence. Its domed shape is like half a pumpkin (*zucca* in Italian) and it is decorated with alternate brown and white segments, like the cupola of Florence cathedral.

1 Heat the oven to 200°C/400°F/Gas Mark 6. Put the almonds and hazelnuts on separate baking trays and toast in the oven for 5 minutes. Then, with a rough towel, rub off as much of the hazelnut skins as you can. Roughly chop the almonds and hazelnuts and set aside.

2 Mix the three liqueurs together. Line the inside of a 1.5l/2½pt pudding basin with cling film and then with cake slices, reserving some for the top. Moisten the cake with most of the liqueur mixture.

3 Melt 60g/2oz of the chocolate in a small bowl set over a pan of simmering water; set aside. Cut the remaining chocolate into small pieces.

4 Whip the cream with the icing sugar until stiff. Fold in the almonds, hazelnuts and chocolate pieces.

5 Divide the cream mixture in half and spoon one portion into the mould, spreading it evenly all over the cake lining the bottom and sides. Fold the melted chocolate into the remaining cream mixture and spoon it into the mould to fill the cavity. Cover the pudding with the reserved cake and moisten it with the rest of the liqueur. Cover the mould with cling film and refrigerate for at least 12 hours.

6 To unmould, place a piece of greaseproof paper and then a piece of cardboard over the top of the pudding basin. Turn the basin over to turn out the pudding on to the paper and cardboard.

Place on a board, remove the basin and peel off the cling film.

7 To decorate the pudding, cut out a circle of greaseproof paper 37cm/15in in diameter. Fold in two to make a half moon, then fold this in two to make a triangle. Fold the triangle in two again to make a thinner triangle. Open out and cut out each alternate section, without cutting the paper through at the top.

8 Dust the whole dome with some sifted icing sugar. Mix 2 tbsp of sifted icing sugar with the cocoa. Place the cut-out circle of paper over the dome and sprinkle the cocoa and sugar mixture in the cut-out sections. Remove the paper carefully without spoiling the pattern. Transfer the pudding to a flat round serving dish, using the cardboard for support. Serve chilled.

ZUPPA INGLESE

CAKE AND CUSTARD PUDDING

Serves 6

150ml/¼pt double cream
350g/¾lb best Madeira cake, cut
into 5mm/¼in slices
4 tbsp rum
4 tbsp cherry brandy
2 egg whites, at room
temperature
5 tbsp icing sugar, sifted
1 tbsp caster sugar

For the custard
500ml/18fl oz full fat milk
2 strips of lemon zest
3 egg yolks
75g/2½oz caster sugar
50g/1¾oz plain flour

Zuppa Inglese used to be on almost every menu in restaurants within Italy and elsewhere, just as Tiramisù is today. And, like Tiramisù, it can be delicious or a disaster. It all depends on the light balance of the ingredients used.

The name Zuppa Inglese – English soup – is a mystery. Like other Italian writers on the subject, I think the pudding must owe its origin to English trifle, which would have been brought to Tuscany and Naples by the English in the eighteenth and nineteenth centuries.

The liqueur Alchermes, used in Italy, is hardly available elsewhere. Cherry brandy is a good substitute.

---

1 First make the custard. Bring the milk to the boil with the lemon zest and set aside.

2 Beat the egg yolks with the sugar until pale yellow and light. Beat the flour into the mixture and then slowly pour in the hot milk.

3 Transfer the custard to a heavy-bottomed saucepan and place over very low heat. Cook, stirring the whole time, until the custard becomes very thick and an occasional bubble breaks through the surface. Simmer very gently for a couple of minutes longer. Place the base of the saucepan in a bowl of iced water to cool the custard quickly. Stir frequently.

4 Whip the cream until soft peaks form. When the custard is cold, fold in the cream.

5 Choose a soufflé dish of 1.75l/2¾pt capacity and line it with greaseproof paper or siliconised baking parchment, which will help in unmoulding the pudding.

6 Line the bottom of the soufflé dish with slices of cake, plugging any holes with pieces of cake. Sprinkle with some rum and spread a couple of spoonsful of custard over the cake.

7 Cover with another layer of cake, moisten it with cherry brandy and then spread over some custard. Repeat these layers, ending with the cake moistened with one of the liqueurs.

8 Cover the pudding with cling film, place it in the refrigerator and chill for at least 8 hours, or better still 24 hours, to allow all the flavours to combine.

9 Some 6 hours before you want to serve the pudding, heat the oven to 110°C/225°F/Gas Mark $\frac{1}{4}$. Whisk the egg whites with the icing sugar until stiff. Remove the pudding from the refrigerator and turn it out on to a round serving dish that can be put in the oven at a low temperature. Spread the meringue all over the pudding and sprinkle with the caster sugar. Bake until the meringue is dry and very pale blond in colour, about $\frac{1}{4}$ hour to 20 minutes. Allow to cool and then replace the pudding in the refrigerator to chill for at least 2 hours before serving.

GELATI, SORBETTI E GELATINE

ICE-CREAMS, SORBETS AND FRUIT JELLIES

I could write a whole book on these sweets, so choosing just a few recipes was quite difficult. Gelati and sorbetti had their origins in Italy, and it was the Italian emigrants who took them to the USA, where people have now adopted them and made them their own.

I find that only in Italy can you still find excellent ices in specialist *gelaterie* – ice-cream shops where the ice-creams are made on the premises. The choice is bewildering. Some new favourite flavours, such as tiramisù and zuppa inglese, compete with the lovely old classics, gelato al caffè or al limone. The fruit water-ices are the best because of the strong flavour of the fruit, ripened in the hot sun.

Fruit jellies are now making a welcome come-back on the tables of health-conscious people, and I have included two recipes for them at the end of this section.

SPUMONE AL CIOCCOLATO

FROZEN CHOCOLATE CREAM LOAF

Serves 8

150g/5oz bitter chocolate
350ml/12fl oz full fat milk
4 egg yolks
120g/4oz sugar
4 level tsp plain flour
4 tbsp strong espresso coffee
300ml/½pt whipping cream,
very cold
12 amaretti (optional)
120ml/4fl oz Marsala or
medium sherry (optional)

A *spumone* is a kind of soft ice-cream. Spumoni are always moulded in a tin, usually a loaf tin, and served cut into slices like a pâté. This is the recipe for a chocolate spumone of a delicate creamy flavour. You need best quality chocolate with a high cocoa butter content.

This spumone is particularly delicious covered with amaretti that have been lightly soaked in Marsala or sherry.

1 Melt the chocolate in a bain-marie.

2 Heat the milk to simmering point.

3 Meanwhile, beat the egg yolks with the sugar until pale and light. Add the flour and beat well. Slowly pour over the hot milk, while beating constantly. Transfer the custard to a heavy-bottomed saucepan and cook over the lowest heat, stirring constantly, until the custard thickens and some bubbles break on the surface. Cook for a couple of minutes longer, never ceasing to stir.

4 Mix the melted chocolate and the coffee into the custard. Put the base of the saucepan in a basin of cold water to cool the custard quickly. Stir every now and then.

5 Whip the cream. When the custard is cold, fold in the cream.

6 Line a 1.5l/2½pt loaf tin with foil or greaseproof paper. Spoon the mixture into the tin and freeze overnight.

7 Remove from the freezer 1 hour before serving. Unmould on to a rectangular dish and cut into slices to serve.

Note: If you wish to cover the ice-cream with amaretti, briefly dip the biscuits in the Marsala or sherry and lay them over the spumone just before serving.

SEMIFREDDO DI ZABAGLIONE AL CAFFE
FROZEN COFFEE ZABAGLIONE

A 'semifreddo' cannot be frozen hard because of the high sugar content in the meringue. This why it is called 'half-cold'. and why its consistency is so soft and voluptuous.

1 In the upper part of a double boiler or in a heatproof bowl, beat the 5 egg yolks with the caster sugar until pale and forming ribbons. Add the cinnamon and Marsala or sherry and continue beating for a minute or so.

2 Put some water in the lower part of the double boiler or in a saucepan in which the bowl can be placed. Turn the heat on and put in place the top of the double boiler or the bowl containing the egg yolk mixture. Beat the mixture constantly while it heats, until it becomes a soft foamy mass. Remove from the heat and add the coffee. Place in a sink of cold water to cool. Stir the zabaglione every now and then to prevent a skin forming.

3 Whip the cream and fold into the zabaglione lightly but thoroughly.

4 Whisk the egg whites until firm. Gradually add the icing sugar and continue beating until the meringue forms stiff peaks. Fold it 1 or 2 spoonfuls at a time into the egg yolk mixture.

5 Spoon the zabaglione into a glass bowl or individual glasses and freeze overnight.

6 Decorate with coffee beans and blobs of whipped cream before serving.

Serves 6

3 eggs, separated
2 egg yolks
120g/4oz caster sugar
pinch of ground cinnamon
150ml/$\frac{1}{4}$pt Marsala or medium sweet sherry
4 tbsp strong espresso coffee
225ml/8fl oz whipping cream
100g/3$\frac{1}{2}$oz icing sugar, sifted
coffee beans and whipped cream, for decoration

SORBETTO AL MANDARINO
CLEMENTINE SORBET

Serves 4

180g/6oz sugar
pared zest of 1 unwaxed lemon,
without any white pith
pared zest of 1 unwaxed orange,
without any white pith
300ml/½pt freshly squeezed
clementine juice
4tbsp freshly squeezed orange
juice
4 tbsp freshly squeezed lemon
juice
2 tbsp white rum

Unfortunately, tasty mandarin oranges are a fruit of the past. However, the tasteless satsumas seem at last to have given way to the new hybrid, clementines, which have recaptured some of the flavour of the mandarin.

This sorbet can also be made with fresh orange juice to which the juice of a lemon is added.

1 Put the sugar, lemon and orange zest and 300ml/½pt of water in a heavy-bottomed saucepan. Bring slowly to the boil and simmer for 5 minutes. Allow to cool, then strain the syrup.
2 Strain the fruit juices and add to the cold syrup with the rum. Mix well and pour the mixture into an ice-cream machine. Freeze according to the manufacturer's instructions.

CASSATA GELATA
ICED CASSATA

Serves 6–8

600ml/1pt full fat milk
grated zest of 1 unwaxed lemon
5 egg yolks
150g/5oz caster sugar
30g/1oz almonds
30g/1oz pistachio nuts
150ml/¼pt whipping cream
30g/1oz candied fruit or
candied peel, chopped
1 tbsp icing sugar, sifted

This is the original, home-made, recipe for the cassata that is now sold frozen in supermarkets. It is quite a lengthy dish to make but it is easy, even if you do not have an ice-cream machine.

You can substitute bits of best chocolate for the pistachio nuts.

1 Heat the milk to simmering point with the lemon zest.
2 Put the egg yolks and caster sugar in a bowl (metal if possible as this will transmit heat and cold more quickly) and beat until pale and mousse-like. I use a hand-held electric beater. Then

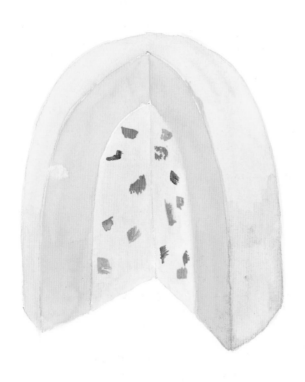

place the bowl over a saucepan of gently simmering water. Add the hot milk while whisking the whole time. Cook until the custard thickens and will coat the back of a spoon. This can easily take as long as 25 minutes. Stir constantly and do not allow the custard to boil or the egg will curdle.

3 As soon as the custard is ready, draw from the heat and set the base of the bowl in a basin of cold water. Allow to cool, stirring frequently. When the custard is cold, strain it to remove the lemon zest, then freeze in an ice-cream machine following the manufacturer's instructions, or still-freeze in the freezer. Do not freeze hard.

4 Place a 1.2l/2pt bombe mould (or a metal mould and a piece of foil to act as a lid) in the freezer to chill for 30 minutes.

5 Spoon the custard ice-cream into the chilled mould, lining the bottom and sides evenly but leaving a hole in the middle. Return the mould to the freezer.

6 Blanch the almonds in boiling water for 30 seconds and then squeeze them in your fingers to remove the skins. Dry and chop them coarsely. Do the same with the pistachio nuts.

7 Whip the cream and fold in the almonds, pistachios, candied fruit, and icing sugar. Spoon this mixture into the centre of the ice-cream lined mould and return it to the freezer. Freeze for at least 4 hours.

8 About an hour before serving, remove the lid from the mould, cover the mould with a flat dish and turn them over. Put the mould, on the dish, in the fridge. By the time you wish to serve the cassata you should be able to lift the mould off easily. If the cassata is still frozen on to the mould, dip the mould quickly into very hot water for a few seconds.

GELATINE DI FRUTTA

FRUIT JELLIES

The image of fruit jellies has been debased by the synthetic-tasting jellies made from packets of jelly powder dissolved in water. In Italy these do not exist; the Italians have always made their jellies from the juice of the fresh fruit. These jellies were particularly popular in the Renaissance, when they were made in various shapes and guises to become the centrepieces of lavishly adorned tables.

Here are two fruit jellies, one for the summer and one for the winter. I use leaf gelatine, not gelatine powder, because it does not have the unpleasant gluey flavour of the powder, and because it dissolves more evenly. Leaf gelatine is sold in the best super-markets and delicatessens.

GELATINA DI ARANCIA

ORANGE JELLY

Serves 4 to 6

20g/¾oz leaf gelatine
150g/5oz sugar
300ml/½pt freshly squeezed
orange juice, strained
4 tbsp freshly squeezed lemon
juice, strained
2 tbsp Grand Marnier
4 tbsp white rum

Buy oranges with full flavour and the right amount of acidity. I use only Italian or Spanish oranges, which have these highly important attributes.

1 Soak the gelatine leaves in cold water for at least 30 minutes.
2 Put the sugar and the strained fruit juices in a saucepan. Bring very slowly to the boil and simmer until the sugar has dissolved, stirring occasionally. Draw off the heat.
3 Put 200ml/7fl oz of water in a saucepan. Lift the gelatine leaves out of the soaking water and squeeze out the liquid. Add to the pan of water and heat gently until the gelatine has dissolved, beating constantly with a small wire balloon whisk. Pour into the fruit syrup and add the two liqueurs. Stir very thoroughly and allow to cool.

4 Grease a 750ml/1¼pt jelly mould with a non-tasting vegetable oil or with almond oil. Pour the mixture into the mould and chill overnight or for at least 6 hours.

5 To turn out, immerse the mould for a few seconds in a basin of warm water. Place a flat dish over the mould and turn the whole thing upside down. Pat the mould and give a few jerks to the dish. the jelly should now turn out easily. Put the mould back on the jelly to cover it and replace the dish in the fridge until ready to serve.

I like to serve this orange jelly with sliced oranges topped with passion fruit. For 4 people you will need 4–5 oranges, 2 tbsp caster sugar and 3 passion fruits. Peel the oranges to the quick and slice very thinly. Put them in a bowl and gently mix in the sugar. Cut the passion fruits in half and with a pointed coffee spoon scoop out the little green seeds and the juice, spreading them all over the orange slices. Make the dish at least 2 hours in advance and keep it refrigerated, covered with cling film.

GELATINA DI MORE O DI RIBES

——— BLACKBERRY OR REDCURRANT JELLY ———

Serves 4–5

20g/$\frac{3}{4}$oz leaf gelatine
120g/4oz sugar
piece of vanilla pod, 5cm/2in
long
300ml/$\frac{1}{2}$pt pure blackberry or
redcurrant juice
4 tbsp Marsala
juice of $\frac{1}{2}$ lemon
150ml/$\frac{1}{4}$pt whipping cream

This is a thick jelly, rich in colour and flavour, suitable for serving in individual bowls. I suggest you make your own fruit juice by boiling the fruit for 2–3 minutes and then straining it through a sieve lined with muslin.

1 Soak the gelatine leaves in cold water for at least 30 minutes.
2 Put the sugar, 100ml/3$\frac{1}{2}$fl oz of water and the vanilla pod in a small saucepan. Bring slowly to the boil, stirring frequently. Simmer for 10 minutes.
3 Squeeze the water out of the gelatine leaves. Add the gelatine to the sugar syrup and allow it to dissolve, while whisking constantly.
4 When the gelatine is thoroughly dissolved draw the pan off the heat. Remove and discard the vanilla pod. Add the fruit juice, Marsala and lemon juice and mix very thoroughly.
5 Spoon the fruit syrup into 4 or 5 bowls. Chill in the refrigerator for at least 6 hours.
6 Whip the cream and drop a spoonful on top of each bowl. Return to the fridge until you are ready to serve the jelly.

LIST OF RECIPES – ANTIPASTI

LIST OF RECIPES – LA PASTA

LIST OF RECIPES – I RISOTTI

LIST OF RECIPES – I DOLCI

FAVOURITE ITALIAN FOOD SHOPS

Salumeria Estense, 837 Fulham Road, London SW6
Valentina, 210 Upper Richmond Road, London SW14
L Terroni, 138-140 Clerkenwell Road, London EC1
Lina Stores, 18 Brewer Street, London W1
Fratelli Camisa, 1 Berwick Street, London W1
G Gazzano & Son, 167-169 Farringdon Road, London EC1
Harvey Nichols, Knightsbridge
Mackintosh of Marlborough, 42a High Street, Marlborough, Wiltshire SN8 1HQ
E H Booth, Old Station, Victoria Street, Windermere, Cumbria LA23 1QA
Mortimer & Bennett, 33 Turnham Green Terrace, London W4
Tom's, 226 Westbourne Grove, London W11
Comestibles, Knock Hundred Row, Midhurst, West Sussex
Jaquest Promotions, Spectrum House, 21 Station Road, Bolsover, Nr Chesterfield
Kendalls, Dean Street, Southgate, Manchester M60 3AU
Todderstaffes Delicatessen, 13 Park Street, Lytham, Lancashire FY8 5LU
Windrush Wines, The Ox House, Market Square, Northleach, Cheltenham, Glos
Valvona & Crolla, 19 Elm Row, Edinburgh EH7 4AA